でる順
パス単

文部科学省後援
英検 **3**級

旺文社

英検とは

　文部科学省後援　実用英語技能検定（通称：英検）は，1963年に第1回試験が実施されて以来，社会教育的な役割という発足当初からの目的と日本社会の国際化が進展するに伴い，英語の四技能「読む・聞く・話す・書く」を総合的に測定する全国規模の試験としてその社会的評価はますます高まっております。

　2011年7月，文部科学省が発表した「国際共通語としての英語力向上のための5つの提言と具体的施策」の中では，中学卒業段階での英語力を英検3級程度以上，高校卒業段階で準2級から2級程度以上を目標とすると明言しており，指導する英語教師も準1級程度以上の英語力を要すると謳っております。

　このように英検の資格はいつの時代も日本人の英語力を測るスケールとして活用されており，大学入試や高校入試での優遇や英語科目の単位として認定する学校が年々増えております。

　また，海外においても英検資格が認知され始め，現在，アメリカやオーストラリアなど多くの大学で留学要件として認められております。

　受験者の皆さんは自己の英語能力の評価基準として，また国際化時代を生きる"国際人"たり得る資格として，さらには生涯学習の目標として大いに英検にチャレンジしてください。

試験概要

(1) 実施機関

　　試験を実施しているのは，公益財団法人 日本英語検定協会です。ホームページ https://www.eiken.or.jp/ では，試験に関する情報を見たり，英検を入試等で活用している学校を検索したりできます。

(2) 試験日程

　　試験は年3回行われます（二次試験は3級以上）。
　　第1回検定：一次試験 ― 5〜6月／二次試験 ― 6〜7月
　　第2回検定：一次試験 ― 10月／二次試験 ― 11月
　　第3回検定：一次試験 ― 1月／二次試験 ― 2〜3月

※受験の際には，英検ウェブサイト等で最新情報をご確認ください。

はじめに

本書は英検合格を目指す皆さんが,「出題される可能性の高い単語を,効率よく覚えられる」ような単語集として,1998年に誕生した「英検Pass単熟語」の4訂版です。

今回の改訂では,以下の3つが本書の特長になります。

3つの特長

❶「でる順」で効果的に覚えられる!
過去5年間の英検問題を分析し,よく出題される単熟語を「でる順」に掲載しました。

❷ すべての見出し語に用例つき!
それぞれの見出し語はすべて用例つきなので,どのように見出し語が使われるかがわかります。

❸ 単熟語暗記のサポートつき!
まとめて覚えたり,書き込んで覚えたりできる別冊「MY WORD BOOK」がついています。くり返し読んで暗記しましょう!

本書での単語学習が皆さんの英検合格につながることを心より願っています。

最後に,本書の刊行にあたり多大なご協力をいただきました,入江泉先生(IWC NEW ZEALAND Ltd.)に深く感謝の意を表します。

もくじ

本書の利用法 …………………………… 6
音声ダウンロードについて …………… 8

単語編　　でる度 Ⓐ 常にでる基本単語

動詞 ………………………………………… 10
名詞 ………………………………………… 19
形容詞・副詞・その他 …………………… 37
チェックテスト …………………………… 49

でる度 Ⓑ よくでる重要単語

動詞 ………………………………………… 52
名詞 ………………………………………… 60
形容詞・副詞・その他 …………………… 81
チェックテスト …………………………… 91

でる度 Ⓒ 差がつく応用単語

動詞 ………………………………………… 94
名詞 ………………………………………… 103
形容詞・副詞・その他 …………………… 124
チェックテスト …………………………… 134
過去問にチャレンジ！① ………………… 136

| 熟語編 | でる度 Ⓐ よくでる重要熟語 | 138 |

チェックテスト ………………………… 163

| | でる度 Ⓑ 差がつく応用熟語 | 166 |

チェックテスト ………………………… 192
過去問にチャレンジ！ ② ……………… 194

| 会話表現編 | 会話表現 | 196 |

チェックテスト ………………………… 213

さくいん ………………………………… 215

でちゃうくん
「でる順」をコンセプトとする問題集に登場する旺文社のキャラクターです。本書の中でも，形がさまざまに変化していきます。『英検でる順合格問題集』（2011年刊行）で誕生しました。

本書とともに，別冊MY WORD BOOK（32p：「まとめて覚えよう！」「書いて覚えよう！」収録）も活用して効果的に学習しましょう。

編集協力：株式会社交学社，山崎召二
本文デザイン：伊藤幸恵　イラスト：三木謙次
装丁デザイン：及川真咲デザイン事務所（浅海新菜）
録音：有限会社スタジオ ユニバーサル
ナレーション：Jack Merluzzi，Bianca Allen，日野まり

本書の利用法

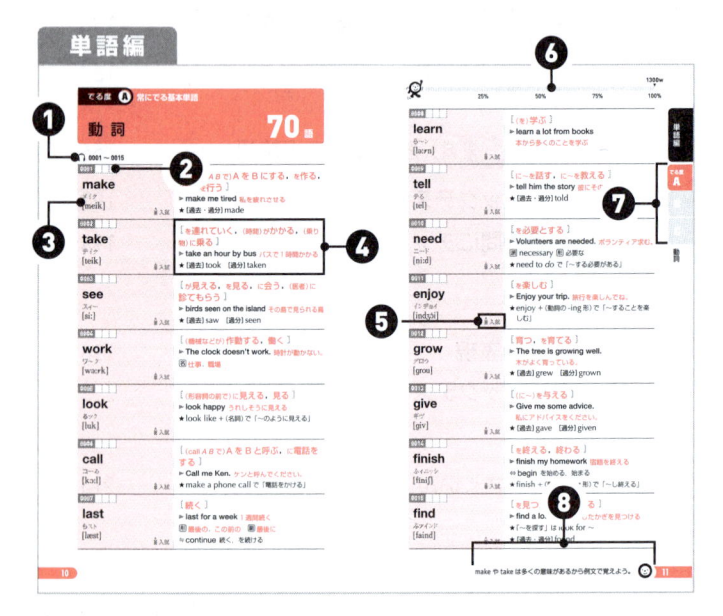

単語編

❶ **音声ダウンロードファイル**：表示の見出し語番号が１つのファイルです。（音声ダウンロードの詳しい内容はp.8を参照してください）

❷ **チェック欄**：チェックしてくり返し学習しましょう。

❸ **発音記号**：発音記号は原則として『マイスタディ英和辞典』（旺文社）に準拠しており，主に米音を採用しています。

❹ **語義その他**：見出し語の語義は英検合格に必要なものを取り上げています。その他，見出し語の反意語（⇔），派生語，用例（▶）などを掲載しています。（動詞の訳に「を」「に」などがあれば他動詞，なければ自動詞です）

❺ **高校入試**：見出し語の中で高校の入学試験によくでるものにはそれぞれ表示（🔑入試）がされています。

❻ **ゲージ**：「単語編＋熟語編」の総語数のうち，どれだけ進んだかがひと目でわかります。

❼ **でる度**：英検問題のデータ分析から出題頻度の高い単語を頻度順に「でる度A，B，C」に分けて掲載しています。

❽ **でちゃうくん**：でちゃうくんが見出し語のちょっとした豆知識について教えてくれます。

本書は，英検3級に出題されやすい単語や熟語などを短期間で効率的に学べるように構成されています。このページで使い方を確認してから，学習をすすめましょう。

本書についている赤セルシートをページの上に載せると，赤で印刷されている部分が隠れるので，覚えるのに効果的です。

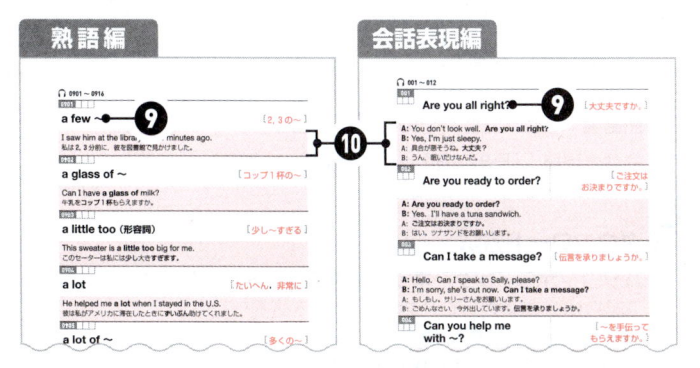

熟語編

🎧 0901 ~ 0916

0901
a few ❾　〔2, 3の～〕

I saw him at the libra____ minutes ago.
私はる，3分前に，彼を図書館で見かけました。

0902
a glass of ~　〔コップ1杯の～〕

Can I have a glass of milk?
牛乳をコップ1杯もらえますか。

0903
a little too（形容詞）　〔少し～すぎる〕

This sweater is a little too big for me.
このセーターは私には少し大きすぎます。

0904
a lot　〔たいへん，非常に〕

He helped me a lot when I stayed in the U.S.
彼はものがアメリカに滞在したときにずいぶん助けてくれました。

0905
a lot of ~　〔多くの～〕

会話表現編

🎧 001 ~ 012

001
Are you all right? ❾　〔大丈夫ですか。〕

A: You don't look well. Are you all right?
B: Yes, I'm just sleepy.
A: 具合が悪そうね。大丈夫？
B: うん。眠いだけなんだ。

002
Are you ready to order?　〔ご注文はお決まりですか。〕

A: Are you ready to order?
B: Yes. I'll have a tuna sandwich.
A: ご注文はお決まりですか。
B: はい，ツナサンドをお願いします。

003
Can I take a message?　〔伝言を承りましょうか。〕

A: Hello. Can I speak to Sally, please?
B: I'm sorry, she's out now. Can I take a message?
A: もしもし，サリーさんをお願いします。
B: ごめんなさい，今外出しています。伝言を承りましょうか。

004
Can you help me with ~?　〔～を手伝ってもらえますか？〕

❾ **熟語，会話表現**：英検3級でよく出題されるものを取り上げています。熟語は「でる度A，B」に分けて掲載しています。

❿ **例文，会話文**：用法を理解できるように，すべての見出しの熟語に例文，会話表現には会話文を掲載しています。例文，会話文は3級レベルになっています。

見出し語が暗記できているかを確認するために，単語編，熟語編の各でる度の最後には「チェックテスト」（見出し語とその意味を確認するテスト）が，単語編と熟語編の最後には「過去問にチャレンジ！」（英検過去問で見出し語が出題された問題）が用意されています。

表記について

- 動 動詞　　名 名詞　　形 形容詞　　副 副詞　　代 代名詞　　接 接続詞
- 助 助動詞　　前 前置詞　　間 間投詞　　派 派生語
- ≒ / ＝ 類義語・同意語　　▶ 用例（見出し語に関連した用例）
- ⇔ 反意語　　★ 備考（動詞の活用形や見出し語の補足情報など）

音声ダウンロードについて

本書に掲載されている単語編・熟語編・会話表現編の以下の音声が無料でダウンロードできます。

🎧 内容

1. 単語編(見出し語1回・ノーマルバージョン)：[見出し語] ⇒ [日本語訳]
2. 単語編(見出し語2回・じっくりバージョン)：
   [見出し語(1回目)] ⇒ [日本語訳] ⇒ [見出し語(2回目)]
3. 熟語編：[見出し語] ⇒ [日本語訳] ⇒ [例文]
4. 会話表現編：[見出し語] ⇒ [日本語訳] ⇒ [例文]

🎧 ダウンロード方法

1. **パソコンからインターネットで専用サイトにアクセス**
   下記のURLを入力してアクセスし，級を選択してください。
   (※検索エンジンの「検索」欄は不可)

   https://www.obunsha.co.jp/tokuten/passtan/

2. **パスワードを入力**
   画面の指示に従い，下記パスワードを入力して「ログイン」ボタンをクリックしてください。

   パスワード：pass3q (※すべて半角数字もしくは半角アルファベット小文字)

3. **聞きたい音声をダウンロード**
   ダウンロードしたい音声ファイルの「DOWNLOAD」ボタンをクリックし，ダウンロードしてください。
   ※詳細は実際のサイト上の説明をご参照ください。

4. **ファイルを解凍して，オーディオプレーヤーで再生**
   音声ファイルはZIP形式にまとめられた形でダウンロードされますので，解凍後，デジタルオーディオプレーヤーなどでご活用ください。
   ※デジタルオーディオプレーヤーへの音声ファイル転送方法は，各製品の取扱説明書やヘルプをご参照ください。

[注意]
- 音声はMP3ファイル形式となっています。音声の再生にはMP3を再生できる機器などが別途必要です。
- ご使用機器，音声再生ソフト等に関する技術的なご質問は，ハードメーカーもしくはソフトメーカーにお願いいたします。
- 本サービスは予告なく終了されることがあります。

でる度

A

B

C

単語編

常にでる基本単語 300

- 動詞 (70語) ········· 10
- 名詞 (137語) ········· 19
- 形容詞・副詞・その他 (93語) ··· 37
- チェックテスト ········· 49

でる度Aは，必ずと言ってよいほど出題される基本単語です。3級合格のために，まずはここに掲載されている300語をしっかり覚えましょう。

	1周目	2周目	3周目
動	/	/	/
名	/	/	/
形・副・他	/	/	/

でる度 A 常にでる基本単語

動詞 70語

🎧 0001〜0015

0001 make
メイク
[meik]
入試

[(make A B で) A を B にする，を作る，(行為) を行う]
► make me tired 私を疲れさせる
★ [過去・過分] made

0002 take
テイク
[teik]
入試

[を連れていく，(時間) がかかる，(乗り物) に乗る]
► take an hour by bus バスで1時間かかる
★ [過去] took　[過分] taken

0003 see
スィー
[siː]
入試

[が見える，を見る，に会う，(医者) に診てもらう]
► birds seen on the island その島で見られる鳥
★ [過去] saw　[過分] seen

0004 work
ワーク
[wəːrk]
入試

[(機械などが) 作動する，働く]
► The clock doesn't work. 時計が動かない。
图 仕事，職場

0005 look
るック
[luk]
入試

[(形容詞の前で) に見える，見る]
► look happy うれしそうに見える
★ look like + (名詞) で「〜のように見える」

0006 call
コーる
[kɔːl]
入試

[(call A B で) A を B と呼ぶ，に電話をする]
► Call me Ken. ケンと呼んでください。
★ make a phone call で「電話をかける」

0007 last
らスト
[læst]
入試

[続く]
► last for a week 1週間続く
形 最後の，この前の　副 最後に
≒ continue 続く，を続ける

10

0008 learn
ら〜ン [ləːrn] 入試

[(を)学ぶ]
► learn a lot from books
本から多くのことを学ぶ

0009 tell
テル [tel] 入試

[に〜を話す, に〜を教える]
► tell him the story 彼にその話をする
★ [過去・過分] told

0010 need
ニード [niːd] 入試

[を必要とする]
► Volunteers are needed. ボランティア求む。
派 necessary 形 必要な
★ need to do で「〜する必要がある」

0011 enjoy
インヂョイ [indʒɔ́i] 入試

[を楽しむ]
► Enjoy your trip. 旅行を楽しんでね。
★ enjoy + (動詞の -ing 形)で「〜することを楽しむ」

0012 grow
グロウ [grou] 入試

[育つ, を育てる]
► The tree is growing well.
木がよく育っている。
★ [過去] grew　[過分] grown

0013 give
ギヴ [giv] 入試

[(に〜)を与える]
► Give me some advice.
私にアドバイスをください。
★ [過去] gave　[過分] given

0014 finish
ふィニッシ [fíniʃ] 入試

[を終える, 終わる]
► finish my homework 宿題を終える
⇔ begin を始める, 始まる
★ finish + (動詞の -ing 形)で「〜し終える」

0015 find
ふァインド [faind] 入試

[を見つける, とわかる]
► find a lost key なくしたかぎを見つける
★ 「〜を探す」は look for 〜
★ [過去・過分] found

make や take は多くの意味があるから例文で覚えよう。

0016 move
ムーヴ [muːv] 入試

[移り住む, 動く, を感動させる]
▶ move to England イングランドへ移り住む

0017 send
センド [send] 入試

[を送る]
▶ send an e-mail Eメールを送る
★ [過去・過分] sent

0018 bring
ブリング [briŋ] 入試

[を持って[連れて]くる, を持って[連れて]いく]
▶ Bring your own lunch. 昼食を持参すること。
★ [過去・過分] brought

0019 try
トゥライ [trai] 入試

[(を)試みる, 試す, 〜しようとする ⟨to do⟩]
▶ try a new shop 新しくできた店に行ってみる

0020 decide
ディサイド [disáid] 入試

[(を)決める, 〜することにする ⟨to do⟩]
▶ decide to go 行くことにする
派 decision 图 決意, 決定

0021 hope
ホウプ [houp] 入試

[を望む]
▶ I hope you like it.
気に入ってくれるといいな。
图 希望, 望み

0022 travel
トゥラヴ(ェ)る [trǽv(ə)l] 入試

[旅行する]
▶ travel around the world 世界中を旅する
图 旅行
≒ trip 旅行

0023 invite
インヴァイト [inváit] 入試

[を招待する]
▶ invite him to the party
彼をパーティーに招待する
★ invite A to B の形でよく使う

0024 join
ヂョイン [dʒɔin] 入試
[(に)参加する，加わる]
► join the team そのチームに加わる

0025 plant
プラント [plænt] 入試
[を植える]
► plant trees 木を植える
名 植物

0026 show
ショウ [ʃou] 入試
[を見せる，に〜を見せる]
► Show me your passport.
パスポートを見せてください。
名 ショー，(テレビの) 番組

0027 become
ビカム [bikʌ́m] 入試
[になる]
► become famous 有名になる
★ 後に形容詞や名詞が続く
★ [過去] became　[過分] become

0028 hold
ホウルド [hould] 入試
[(会など)を開く]
► the concert held on Sunday
日曜日に開かれるコンサート
★ [過去・過分] held

0029 rain
レイン [rein] 入試
[雨が降る]
► It's raining. 雨が降っている。
名 雨
派 rainy 形 雨降りの

0030 win
ウィン [win] 入試
[(に)勝つ，を勝ち取る]
► win a game 試合に勝つ
⇔ lose (に)負ける
★ [過去・過分] won

0031 put
プット [put] 入試
[を置く]
► put it on the desk それを机の上に置く
★ put 〜 in [into] … は「〜を…に入れる」
★ [過去・過分] put

0032
wear
ウェア
[weər]
入試

[を身につけている]
▶ the boy wearing a cap
帽子をかぶっている男の子
★ [過去] wore　[過分] worn

0033
keep
キープ
[ki:p]
入試

[(keep -ing で)〜し続ける，を(ある状態)にしておく]
▶ keep talking 話し続ける
★ [過去・過分] kept

0034
sound
サウンド
[saund]
入試

[(形容詞の前で)に聞こえる]
▶ That sounds good. それはいいね。
名 音
★ sound like+(名詞)で「〜のように聞こえる」

0035
speak
スピーク
[spi:k]
入試

[(を)話す]
▶ speak in English 英語で話す
派 speech 名 スピーチ，演説
★ [過去] spoke　[過分] spoken

0036
build
ビルド
[bild]
入試

[を建てる，を造る]
▶ a house built in the 17th century
17世紀に建てられた家
★ [過去・過分] built

0037
clean
クリーン
[kli:n]
入試

[をきれいにする]
▶ clean the blackboard 黒板をきれいにする
形 きれいな，清潔な
⇔ dirty 汚い，汚れた

0038
drive
ドゥライヴ
[draiv]
入試

[を運転する，(人)を車で送る]
▶ drive him to school
彼を学校まで車で送る
★ [過去] drove　[過分] driven

0039
happen
ハプン
[hæp(ə)n]
入試

[起こる]
▶ What happened to him?
彼に何が起こったのか。
派 happening 名 できごと，事件

0040
remember
リメンバァ
[rimémbər]
入試

[(を)思い出す, (を)覚えている]
▶ I can't remember his name.
彼の名前を思い出せない。
⇔ forget (を)忘れる

0041
return
リターン
[ritə́ːrn]
入試

[を返す, 戻る]
▶ return a book to the library
図書館に本を返す
≒ go back 戻る

0042
say
セイ
[sei]
入試

[と書いてある, と言う]
▶ The sign says: NO FOOD OR DRINK.
看板に「飲食禁止」と書いてある。
★ [過去・過分] said

0043
sleep
スリープ
[sliːp]
入試

[眠る]
▶ sleep on the floor 床で寝る
名 睡眠, 眠り 派 sleepy 形 眠い
★ [過去・過分] slept

0044
paint
ペイント
[peint]
入試

[にペンキを塗る, を絵の具で描く]
▶ paint the wall 壁にペンキを塗る
名 絵の具, ペンキ
派 painting 名 絵, 絵を描くこと

0045
watch
ワ(ー)ッチ
[wɑ(ː)tʃ]
入試

[を(注意して)見る]
▶ watch a game on TV テレビで試合を見る
名 腕時計

0046
worry
ワ〜リィ
[wə́ːri]
入試

[心配する, を心配させる]
▶ Don't worry. 心配しないで。
★ be worried about 〜で「〜を心配する」

0047
save
セイヴ
[seiv]
入試

[を貯える, を節約する, を救う]
▶ save enough money to buy a new bike
新しい自転車を買うのに十分なお金を貯める

---

wear は身につけている状態, put on は身につける動作を表すよ。

0048
sell
セる
[sel]
入試

[を売る]
▶ sell old books 古本を売る
⇔ buy を買う
★ [過去・過分] sold

0049
snow
スノウ
[snou]
入試

[雪が降る]
▶ It's snowing. 雪が降っている。
名 雪
派 snowy 形 雪の多い，雪の積もった

0050
understand
アンダスタンド
[ʌ̀ndərstǽnd]
入試

[(を)理解する]
▶ understand the meaning 意味を理解する
★ [過去・過分] understood

0051
begin
ビギン
[bigín]
入試

[を始める，始まる]
▶ The war began. 戦争が始まった。
⇔ finish を終える，終わる
★ [過去] began [過分] begun

0052
borrow
ボーロウ
[bɔ́:rou]
入試

[を借りる]
▶ borrow a book from the library
図書館から本を借りる
⇔ lend を貸す

0053
cover
カヴァ
[kʌ́vər]
入試

[をおおう]
▶ The mountain is covered with snow.
その山は雪でおおわれている。
名 表紙，カバー

0054
miss
ミス
[mis]
入試

[に乗り遅れる，がいなくてさびしく思う]
▶ miss the last train 最終電車を逃す

0055
wait
ウェイト
[weit]
入試

[待つ ⟨for ～ ～を⟩]
▶ wait for the next bus 次のバスを待つ

0056
arrive
アライヴ
[əráiv] 🔒入試

[到着する]
▶ arrive at the airport 空港に着く
≒ get to ～ ～に着く

0057
break
ブレイク
[breik] 🔒入試

[を壊す, を割る]
▶ I broke his cup. 彼のコップを割った。
★ broken は形容詞「壊れた」でもよく使う
★ [過去] broke [過分] broken

0058
change
チェインヂ
[tʃeindʒ] 🔒入試

[を変える, 変わる]
▶ change a plan 計画を変更する
图 おつり

0059
choose
チューズ
[tʃu:z] 🔒入試

[(を)選ぶ]
▶ choose the best way 最良の方法を選ぶ
★ [過去] chose [過分] chosen

0060
graduate
グラヂュエイト
[grǽdʒueit]

[卒業する〈from ～ ～を〉]
▶ graduate from university 大学を卒業する
派 graduation 图 卒業, 卒業式

0061
leave
リーヴ
[li:v] 🔒入試

[を置き忘れる, (を)出発する, を残す]
▶ leave a book on a train
本を電車に置き忘れる
★ [過去・過分] left

0062
lend
レンド
[lend]

[を貸す]
▶ lend her a book 彼女に本を貸す
⇔ borrow を借りる
★ [過去・過分] lent

0063
feel
ふィール
[fi:l] 🔒入試

[(形容詞の前で)に感じる]
▶ I don't feel well. 具合がよくない。
★ [過去・過分] felt

break や leave, feel は過去・過去分詞もよく出るよ。

🎧 0064〜0070

0064
pick
ピック
[pik] 🔒入試

[を摘む，を選ぶ]
▶ pick flowers 花を摘む

0065
receive
リスィーヴ
[risíːv] 🔒入試

[を受け取る]
▶ receive a letter 手紙を受け取る

0066
spend
スペンド
[spend] 🔒入試

[(時間・お金)を費やす]
▶ spend time on the beach
　浜辺で時間を過ごす
★ [過去・過分] spent

0067
bake
ベイク
[beik]

[(パンなど)を焼く]
▶ bake a cake ケーキを焼く

0068
draw
ドゥロー
[drɔː]

[(絵・図)を描く，(線)を引く]
▶ pictures drawn with a pen ペンで描いた絵
★「(絵の具で)を描く」は paint
★ [過去] drew [過分] drawn

0069
skate
スケイト
[skeit]

[スケートをする]
▶ go skating スケートをしに行く
派 skating 名 スケート(をすること)
★「アイススケート」は ice-skating

0070
turn
ターン
[təːrn] 🔒入試

[(を)曲がる]
▶ turn right 右に曲がる

でる度 A 常にでる基本単語

名詞 137語

0071 ~ 0077

0071
p.m.
ピーエム
[píːém]

[午後]
▶ arrive at 2 p.m. 午後2時に到着する
★「午前」は a.m.

0072
zoo
ズー
[zuː] 入試

[動物園]
▶ go to the zoo 動物園へ行く

0073
animal
アニマる
[ǽnim(ə)l] 入試

[動物]
▶ take care of animals 動物の世話をする

0074
festival
ふェスティヴァる
[féstiv(ə)l]

[祭り]
▶ a summer festival 夏祭り

0075
elephant
エれふァント
[élif(ə)nt]

[ゾウ]
▶ An elephant has big ears.
ゾウには大きな耳がある。

0076
date
デイト
[deit]

[日付]
▶ What's the date today? 今日は何日ですか。
★「今日は何曜日ですか」は What day is it today?

0077
subject
サブヂェクト
[sʌ́bdʒekt] 入試

[教科, （Eメールなどの）件名]
▶ Subject: Thanks! 件名：ありがとう！

お疲れさま！ このページからは名詞だよ。

0078
store
ストー
[stɔːr]
入試

[店]
▶ a toy store おもちゃ屋
= shop

0079
a.m.
エイエム
[èiém]

[午前]
▶ That shop opens at 9 a.m.
その店は午前9時に開店する。
★「午後」は p.m.

0080
toy
トイ
[tɔi]

[おもちゃ]
▶ This is a child's toy.
これは子ども用のおもちゃだよ。

0081
movie
ムーヴィ
[múːvi]
入試

[映画]
▶ watch a movie on TV テレビで映画を見る
= film

0082
weekend
ウィーケンド
[wíːkend]

[週末]
▶ this weekend 今週末(に)
★「平日」は weekday

0083
contest
カ(ー)ンテスト
[káː(ː)ntest]

[コンテスト]
▶ a speech contest スピーチコンテスト

0084
money
マニィ
[mʌ́ni]
入試

[お金]
▶ save money お金を貯める

0085
restaurant
レストラント
[réstərənt]
入試

[レストラン]
▶ a Chinese restaurant 中華料理店

0086
trip
トゥリップ
[trip]
入試

[旅行]
► How was the trip to France?
フランスへの旅行はどうでしたか。
≒ travel 旅行

0087
information
インふォメイション
[ìnfərméiʃ(ə)n]
入試

[情報]
► information on the Internet
インターネット上の情報

0088
kind
カインド
[kaind]
入試

[種類]
► many kinds of birds 多くの種類の鳥
形 親切な

0089
dictionary
ディクショネリィ
[díkʃəneri]

[辞書]
► Can I use your dictionary?
君の辞書を借りてもいい?

0090
food
ふード
[fu:d]
入試

[食べ物, 料理]
► Chinese food 中華料理
派 feed 動 に食べ物を与える

0091
doctor
ダ(ー)クタァ
[dá(:)ktər]
入試

[医師]
► go to the doctor 医者に診てもらいに行く
★「看護師」は nurse

0092
job
ヂャ(ー)ップ
[dʒɑ(:)b]
入試

[仕事]
► look for a job 仕事を探す

0093
kitten
キトゥン
[kít(ə)n]

[子猫]
► find a kitten at the park
公園で子猫を見つける
★「子犬」は puppy

information や dictionary などの長い語は書いて覚えよう。

0094
university
ユーニヴァ〜スィティ
[jùːnivə́ːrsəti]
入試

[（総合）大学]
► study history at university
大学で歴史を勉強する
≒ college（単科）大学

0095
part
パート
[pɑːrt]
入試

[部分]
► the southern part of the U.S.
アメリカ合衆国の南部

0096
place
プレイス
[pleis]
入試

[場所]
► a lot of places to visit
訪れるべき多くの場所

0097
fun
ふァン
[fʌn]
入試

[楽しいこと]
► It was a lot of fun. とても楽しかった。

0098
parent
ペ（ア）レント
[pé(ə)r(ə)nt]
入試

[親]
► go hiking with my parents
両親とハイキングに行く
★複数形 parents で「両親」

0099
vacation
ヴェイケイション
[veikéiʃ(ə)n]
入試

[休暇]
► during the winter vacation
冬休みの間(に，中)

0100
volunteer
ヴァ(ー)らンティア
[vɑ̀(ː)ləntíər]
入試

[ボランティア（をする人）]
► as a volunteer ボランティアとして
★volunteer は人を指し，「ボランティア活動」は volunteer activity [work]

0101
band
バンド
[bænd]

[（音楽の）バンド]
► play the guitar in a band
バンドでギターを弾く
★music band とは言わない

0102
chimpanzee
チンパンズィー
[tʃìmpænzíː]

[チンパンジー]
▶ study chimpanzees
チンパンジーを研究する
★「サル」は monkey

0103
library
らイブレリィ
[láibreri]
🔒入試

[図書館]
▶ go to the library to borrow books
本を借りに図書館へ行く
派 librarian 名 図書館員

0104
plan
プらン
[plæn]
🔒入試

[予定，計画]
▶ plans for tomorrow 明日の予定
動 を計画する

0105
e-mail
イーメイる
[íːmeil]
🔒入試

[E メール]
▶ write an e-mail Eメールを書く

0106
hour
アウア
[áuər]
🔒入試

[(1) 時間]
▶ an hour ago 1時間前に

0107
practice
プラクティス
[præktis]
🔒入試

[練習]
▶ go to tennis practice テニスの練習に行く
動 を練習する

0108
son
サン
[sʌn]
🔒入試

[息子]
▶ He's proud of his son.
彼は息子を誇りに思っている。
⇔ daughter 娘

0109
country
カントゥリィ
[kʌ́ntri]
🔒入試

[国，(the country で)いなか]
▶ live in the country いなかに住む

0110
meeting
ミーティング
[míːtiŋ]
入試

[会合，会議]
▶ the meeting held on Friday
金曜日に開かれる会合

0111
newspaper
ヌーズペイパァ
[núːzpèipər]
入試

[新聞]
▶ read a newspaper 新聞を読む
★ 単に paper とも言う

0112
scientist
サイエンティスト
[sáiəntəst]
入試

[科学者]
▶ a famous scientist 有名な科学者
派 science 名 理科，科学

0113
stop
スタ(ー)ップ
[stɑ(ː)p]
入試

[(バスの)停留所]
▶ Get off at the next stop.
次の停留所で降りてください。
動 を止める，止まる

0114
area
エ(ア)リア
[é(ə)riə]
入試

[地域，区域]
▶ a parking area 駐車区域

0115
aunt
アント
[ænt]
入試

[おば]
▶ an aunt working in Sydney
シドニーで働いているおば
⇔ uncle おじ

0116
company
カンパニィ
[kʌ́mp(ə)ni]
入試

[会社]
▶ a computer company コンピューター会社

0117
cookie
クッキィ
[kúki]

[クッキー]
▶ bake cookies クッキーを焼く

24

0118 farmer
ふァーマァ [fáːrmər] 🔒入試

[農場経営者, 農家]
► farmers in my town 私の町の農家
派 farm 名 農場

0119 garden
ガードゥン [gáːrd(ə)n] 🔒入試

[庭]
► clean the garden 庭を掃除する

0120 idea
アイディ(ー)ア [aidí(ː)ə] 🔒入試

[考え, アイデア]
► I have an idea. 私に考えがあります。

0121 lesson
れスン [lés(ə)n] 🔒入試

[授業, けいこ]
► go to dance lessons
　ダンスのけいこに行く

0122 medicine
メドゥス(ィ)ン [méds(ə)n] 🔒入試

[薬]
► take medicine 薬を飲む

0123 month
マンす [mʌnθ] 🔒入試

[(暦の上の)月]
► six months later 半年後に

0124 pumpkin
パン(プ)キン [pʌ́m(p)kin]

[カボチャ]
► pumpkin soup カボチャのスープ

0125 space
スペイス [speis] 🔒入試

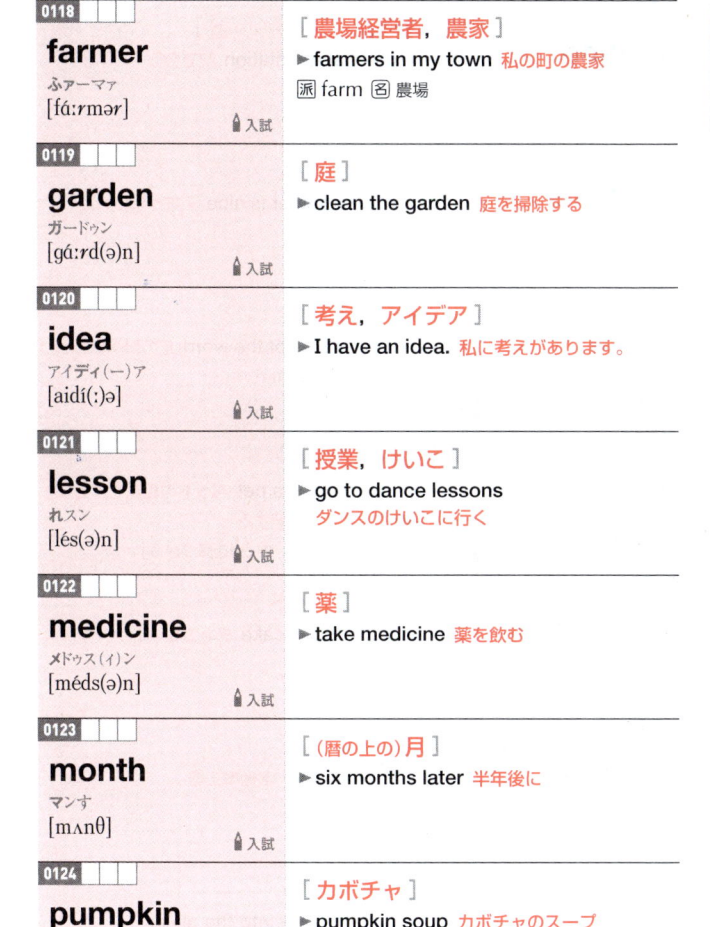

[宇宙, 空間]
► go to space 宇宙へ行く

scientist の -ist や farmer の -er は「人」を表すよ。

0126
station
ステイション
[stéiʃ(ə)n]
入試

[駅，(警察や消防の)署]
▶ meet at the station 駅で会う

0127
weather
ウェざァ
[wéðər]
入試

[天気]
▶ if the weather is nice 天気がよければ

0128
word
ワ〜ド
[wəːrd]
入試

[単語]
▶ the spelling of the word その単語のつづり
★「文」は sentence

0129
care
ケア
[keər]
入試

[世話，注意]
▶ take care of a pet ペットの世話をする
動 気にする，心配する
★care about 〜 で「〜を気づかう」

0130
chocolate
チョークれット
[tʃɔ́ːklət]

[チョコレート]
▶ a chocolate cake チョコレートケーキ

0131
factory
ふァクトリィ
[fǽkt(ə)ri]

[工場]
▶ a car factory 自動車工場

0132
ice
アイス
[ais]
入試

[氷]
▶ put some ice into the glass
コップに氷を入れる

0133
pizza
ピーツァ
[píːtsə]

[ピザ]
▶ a piece of pizza 1切れのピザ

0134
prize
プライズ
[praiz]

[賞]
► win a prize 賞をとる
≒ award 賞

0135
report
リポート
[ripɔ́ːrt]

[報告(書), レポート]
► write a report about space
宇宙に関するレポートを書く
動 を報告する

0136
street
ストリート
[striːt]
入試

[通り]
► walk down the street 通りを歩く

0137
visitor
ヴィズィタァ
[vízətər]

[訪問者]
► visitors to the zoo 動物園を訪れる人たち

0138
way
ウェイ
[wei]
入試

[方法, 方向]
► the best way to learn English
英語を学ぶ最もよい方法

0139
concert
カ(ー)ンサト
[ká(ː)nsərt]
入試

[演奏会]
► a piano concert ピアノの演奏会

0140
cousin
カズン
[kʌ́z(ə)n]

[いとこ]
► a cousin who lives in New York
ニューヨークに住んでいるいとこ

0141
doghouse
ド(ー)グハウス
[dɔ́(ː)ghaus]

[犬小屋]
► how to make a doghouse 犬小屋の作り方

0142
group
グループ
[gru:p]
入試

[団体，グループ]
▶ a volunteer group ボランティアグループ

0143
history
ヒストリィ
[híst(ə)ri]
入試

[歴史]
▶ a history test 歴史のテスト

0144
letter
れタァ
[létər]
入試

[文字，手紙]
▶ letters on the sign 看板に書かれた文字

0145
minute
ミニット
[mínit]
入試

[ちょっとの間，（1）分]
▶ wait a minute ちょっとの間待つ

0146
musician
ミュズィシャン
[mjuzíʃ(ə)n]

[音楽家]
▶ a famous musician 有名な音楽家

0147
notice
ノウティス
[nóutəs]
入試

[掲示，通知]
▶ a notice for parents 親向けの掲示 [通知]
動 に気がつく

0148
thing
すィング
[θiŋ]
入試

[もの，こと]
▶ a lot of things to learn 学ぶべき多くのこと

0149
ticket
ティケット
[tíkət]
入試

[切符，チケット]
▶ a concert ticket コンサートのチケット

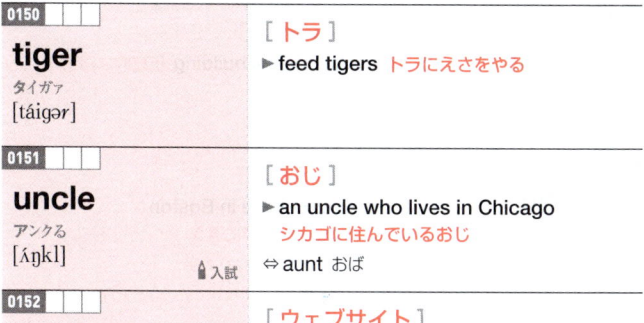

0150 tiger
タイガァ [táigər]

[トラ]
▶ feed tigers トラにえさをやる

0151 uncle
アンクる [ʌ́ŋkl] 入試

[おじ]
▶ an uncle who lives in Chicago シカゴに住んでいるおじ
⇔ aunt おば

0152 website
ウェブサイト [wébsait]

[ウェブサイト]
▶ visit the website ウェブサイトを見る

0153 floor
ふろー [flɔːr] 入試

[(建物の)階, 床]
▶ on the fifth floor 5階に

0154 life
らいふ [laif] 入試

[一生, 生活, 命]
▶ a book about his life 彼の生涯についての本
★ [複数形] lives

0155 office
ア(ー)ふぃス [á(:)fəs] 入試

[事務所, オフィス]
▶ a post office 郵便局

0156 pool
プーる [puːl]

[(スイミング)プール]
▶ swim in a pool プールで泳ぐ

0157 winner
ウィナァ [wínər]

[勝利者, 優勝者]
▶ the winner of the contest そのコンテストの優勝者

0158
building
ビるディング
[bíldiŋ]
入試

[建物，ビル]
▶ a traditional building 伝統的な建物

0159
college
カ(ー)れッヂ
[ká(:)lidʒ]
入試

[(単科)大学]
▶ go to college in Boston
ボストンの大学に通う
≒ university （総合）大学

0160
daughter
ドータァ
[dɔ́:tər]
入試

[娘]
▶ She has a daughter. 彼女には娘がいる。
⇔ son 息子

0161
fair
ふェア
[feər]

[見本市，バザー]
▶ sell used clothes at the fair
バザーで古着を売る
形 公平な

0162
French
ふレンチ
[frentʃ]

[フランス語]
▶ learn French フランス語を学ぶ
形 フランス（人[語]）の

0163
future
ふューチャ
[fjú:tʃər]
入試

[未来，将来]
▶ in the future 将来，未来に
⇔ past 過去

0164
government
ガヴァ(ン)メント
[gʌ́vər(n)mənt]

[政府]
▶ the American government アメリカ政府

0165
hospital
ハ(ー)スピトゥる
[há(:)spitl]
入試

[病院]
▶ He is in the hospital. 彼は入院している。

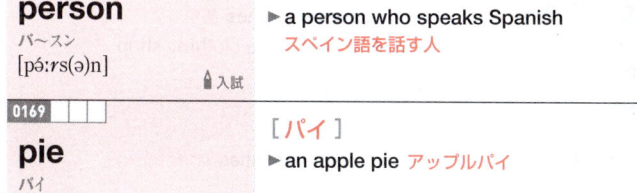

0166
instrument
インストゥルメント
[ínstrəmənt]

[楽器，器具]
▶ a musical instrument 楽器

0167
jazz
ヂャズ
[dʒæz]

[ジャズ(音楽)]
▶ a jazz singer ジャズの歌手
★ jazz music とも言う

0168
person
パ〜スン
[pə́:rs(ə)n]　入試

[人]
▶ a person who speaks Spanish
スペイン語を話す人

0169
pie
パイ
[pai]

[パイ]
▶ an apple pie アップルパイ

0170
Spanish
スパニッシ
[spǽniʃ]

[スペイン語]
▶ in Spanish class スペイン語の授業で
形 スペイン(人[語])の

0171
vegetable
ヴェヂタブる
[védʒtəbl]　入試

[野菜]
▶ grow vegetables 野菜を育てる

0172
wife
ワイふ
[waif]　入試

[妻]
▶ he and his wife 彼とその妻
⇔ husband 夫

0173
writer
ライタァ
[ráitər]　入試

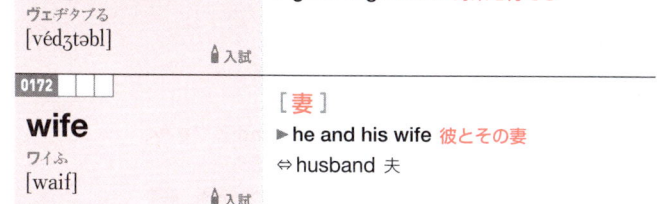

[作家]
▶ She is known as a writer.
彼女は作家として知られている。

France 名 や French 名・形 などはセットで覚えよう。

0174
bookstore
ブックストー
[búkstɔːr]

[書店]
▶ work at a bookstore 書店で働く

0175
camera
キャメラ
[kǽm(ə)rə]

[カメラ]
▶ buy a small camera 小さなカメラを買う

0176
clothes
クロウズ
[klouz] 入試

[衣服]
▶ change clothes 服を着替える
★「衣料品店」は a clothing shop

0177
dish
ディッシ
[diʃ] 入試

[皿, 料理]
▶ wash the dishes 皿を洗う

0178
end
エンド
[end] 入試

[終わり]
▶ at the end of the street 通りの行き止まりに
動 終わる, を終える
⇔ beginning 初め

0179
event
イヴェント
[ivént]

[行事, イベント]
▶ a school event 学校行事

0180
farm
ふアーム
[fɑːrm] 入試

[農場]
▶ work on a farm 農場で働く
派 farming 名 農業
　　farmer 名 農場経営者, 農家

0181
forest
ふォーレスト
[fɔ́ːrəst] 入試

[森林]
▶ in the forest 森の中で

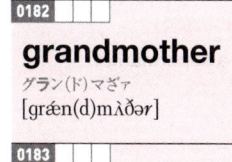

0182 grandmother
グラン(ド)マザァ
[grǽn(d)mʌ̀ðər]

[祖母]
► see my grandmother in the hospital
入院中の祖母を見舞いに行く
= grandma ⇔ grandfather 祖父

0183 island
アイらンド
[áilənd] 🔒入試

[島]
► stay on an island 島に滞在する

0184 magazine
マガズィーン
[mǽgəzi:n]

[雑誌]
► a baseball magazine 野球雑誌

0185 member
メンバァ
[mémbər] 🔒入試

[一員]
► a member of the tennis club
テニス部の一員

0186 message
メセッヂ
[mésidʒ] 🔒入試

[伝言]
► leave a message 伝言を残す

0187 nature
ネイチャ
[néitʃər] 🔒入試

[自然]
► in nature 自然界で
派 natural 形 自然の
★ nature は海や陸,動植物などを含む

0188 road
ロウド
[roud] 🔒入試

[道, 道路]
► cross the road 道路を横切る

0189 speech
スピーチ
[spi:tʃ] 🔒入試

[スピーチ, 演説]
► make [give] a speech スピーチをする
派 speak 動 (を)話す

0190
supermarket
スーパマーケット
[súːpərmàːrkət]

[スーパーマーケット]
▶ go shopping at a supermarket
スーパーへ買い物に行く

0191
train
トゥレイン
[trein] 入試

[列車, 電車]
▶ take a train 電車に乗る
動 を訓練する

0192
actor
アクタァ
[æktər]

[俳優]
▶ a movie actor 映画俳優
派 actress 图 女優
　　act 動 (を)演じる, 行動する

0193
beach
ビーチ
[biːtʃ] 入試

[浜辺, 海辺]
▶ go to the beach 海(辺)へ行く
★ shore は「岸」全般, coast は「海岸」

0194
color
カらァ
[kʌ́lər] 入試

[色]
▶ Do you have it in another color?
それの別の色のものはありますか。
派 colorful 形 色鮮やかな

0195
convenience
コンヴィーニエンス
[kənvíːniəns]

[便利さ]
▶ a convenience store
コンビニエンスストア
派 convenient 形 便利な

0196
culture
カるチャ
[kʌ́ltʃər] 入試

[文化]
▶ a different culture 異文化

0197
god
ガ(ー)ッド
[gɑ(ː)d]

[神]
▶ ask a god for help 神に助けを求める

0198
gym
ヂム
[dʒim]

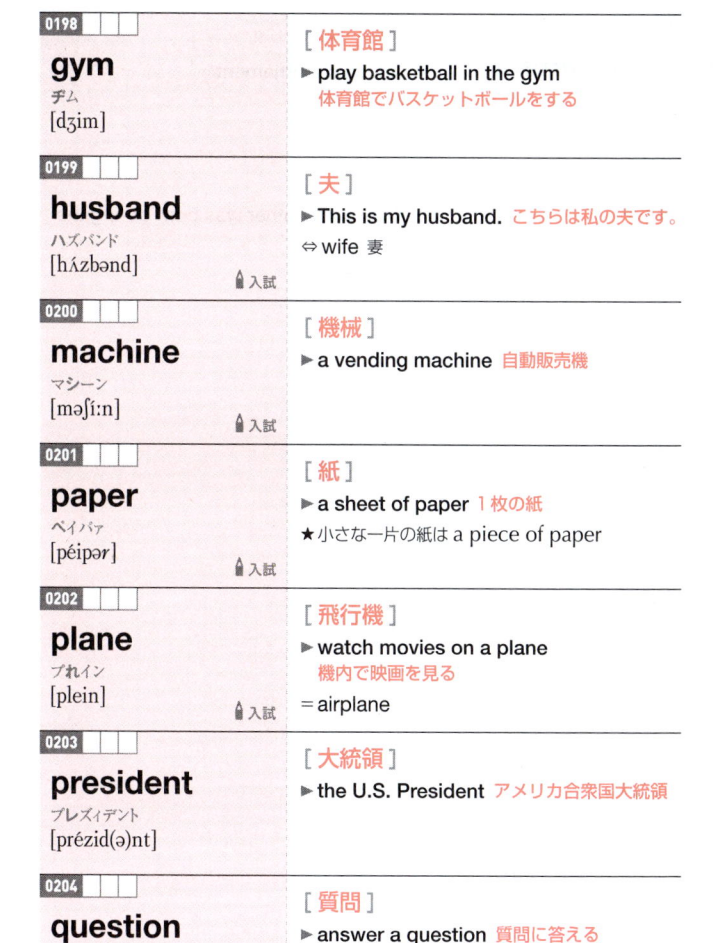

[体育館]
► play basketball in the gym
体育館でバスケットボールをする

0199
husband
ハズバンド
[hʌ́zbənd]

[夫]
► This is my husband. こちらは私の夫です。
⇔ wife 妻

0200
machine
マシーン
[məʃíːn]

[機械]
► a vending machine 自動販売機

0201
paper
ペイパァ
[péipər]

[紙]
► a sheet of paper 1枚の紙
★小さな一片の紙は a piece of paper

0202
plane
プレイン
[plein]

[飛行機]
► watch movies on a plane
機内で映画を見る
= airplane

0203
president
プレズィデント
[prézid(ə)nt]

[大統領]
► the U.S. President アメリカ合衆国大統領

0204
question
クウェスチョン
[kwéstʃ(ə)n]

[質問]
► answer a question 質問に答える

0205
salad
サらッド
[sǽləd]

[サラダ]
► make a salad サラダを作る

actress は女性のことだけど，actor は男女に使うよ。

0206

tournament
トゥアナメント
[túərnəmənt]

[試合, トーナメント]
▶ a tennis tournament
テニスのトーナメント

0207

war
ウォー
[wɔːr]
🔒 入試

[戦争]
▶ My grandmother was born during the war. 祖母は戦争中に生まれました。
⇔ peace 平和

でる度 A 常にでる基本単語

形容詞・副詞・その他 93語

🎧 0208～0214

0208 other
アざァ [ʌ́ðər]
形 [ほかの]
▶ in other countries ほかの国々で

0209 dear
ディア [diər]
形 [(手紙の冒頭で)親愛なる～]
▶ Dear Mr. Smith, 親愛なるスミス先生へ

0210 well
ウェる [wel]
形 [元気な]
▶ You don't look well. 具合が悪そうだね。
副 じょうずに, 十分に　間 ええと, さて

0211 free
ふリー [friː]
形 [無料の, ひまな]
▶ a free drink 無料の飲み物

0212 best
ベスト [best]
形 [(good, well の最上級)最もよい]
▶ the best way いちばんよい方法
副 (well の最上級)最もよく[じょうずに]

0213 famous
ふェイマス [féiməs]
形 [有名な〈for ～ ～で〉]
▶ Our town is famous for its beautiful park.
私たちの町は美しい公園で有名です。

0214 special
スペシャる [spéʃ(ə)l]
形 [特別な]
▶ a special sale 特別セール

お疲れさま！ このページからは形容詞だよ。

0215 little
リトゥる
[lítl]
入試

形 [(a little ~で)少しの~]
► a little water 少しの水
副 (a little で)少し
★数えられる名詞には few を使う

0216 sorry
サ(ー)リィ
[sá(:)ri]
入試

形 [気の毒に思って，申し訳なく思って]
► I'm sorry to hear that.
それはお気の毒です。

0217 better
ベタァ
[bétər]
入試

形 [(good, well の比較級)よりよい]
► a better choice よりよい選択
副 (well の比較級)よりよく[じょうずに]

0218 popular
パ(ー)ピュらァ
[pá(:)pjulər]
入試

形 [人気のある]
► The movie is popular among children.
その映画は子どもたちに人気があります。

0219 right
ライト
[rait]
入試

形 [右の，正しい]
► You're right. そのとおりです。
名 右
副 右に，ちょうど

0220 favorite
ふエイヴ(ァ)リット
[féiv(ə)rət]
入試

形 [お気に入りの，大好きな]
► my favorite singer 私のお気に入りの歌手
名 お気に入りのもの

0221 sick
スィック
[sik]
入試

形 [病気の，気分の悪い]
► visit a sick friend in the hospital
病気で入院中の友人を見舞いに行く
≒ ill 病気の 派 sickness 名 病気

0222 busy
ビズィ
[bízi]
入試

形 [忙しい，混雑した]
► have a busy day 忙しい日を過ごす
★ busy + (動詞の -ing 形)で「~するのに忙しい」

0223 late
レイト [leit] 入試

形 [遅れた〈for ～ ～に〉, 遅い]
► Sorry I'm late. 遅れてごめん。
副 遅く
⇔ early 早い, 早く

0224 most
モウスト [moust] 入試

形 [大部分の]
► most students 大部分の生徒
★many/much の最上級「最も多くの」の意味でも重要。代名詞で most of ～は「～の大部分」

0225 beautiful
ビューティふる [bjúːtəf(ə)l] 入試

形 [美しい]
► beautiful flowers 美しい花
派 beauty 名 美

0226 close
クろウス [klous] 入試

形 [近い, 親密な]
► We were close to each other.
私たちはお互いに近くにいた。

0227 different
ディふ(ァ)レント [díf(ə)r(ə)nt] 入試

形 [異なった, 別の, さまざまな]
► many different countries 多くの異なる国
⇔ same 同じ 派 difference 名 違い
★be different from ～で「～と違う」

0228 enough
イナふ [ináf] 入試

形 [十分な]
► have enough time 十分な時間がある
副 十分に

0229 sure
シュア [ʃuər] 入試

形 [確かな, 確信して]
► Are you sure? 確かですか。
副 (会話で) もちろん

0230 ready
レディ [rédi] 入試

形 [準備ができて]
► Dinner is ready!
夕飯の準備ができたよ！

0231
glad
グラッド
[glæd]
入試

形 [うれしい]
▶ I'm glad to hear that.
それを聞いてうれしい。
≒ happy うれしい, 幸せな　⇔ sad 悲しい

0232
same
セイム
[seim]
入試

形 [同じ]
▶ the same team 同じチーム
⇔ different 異なった, 別の, さまざまな

0233
difficult
ディふィカルト
[dífik(ə)lt]
入試

形 [難しい]
▶ a difficult job 難しい仕事
≒ hard 大変な, つらい, 難しい
⇔ easy 簡単な　派 difficulty 名 困難

0234
fine
ふァイン
[fain]
入試

形 [申し分ない, 晴れた, 元気な]
▶ Any place is fine. どこでもいいです。

0235
Italian
イタリャン
[itǽljən]

形 [イタリア(人[語])の]
▶ an Italian restaurant イタリア料理店
名 イタリア人[語]
派 Italy 名 イタリア

0236
surprised
サプライズド
[sərpráizd]
入試

形 [(人が)驚いた ⟨at ～ ～に⟩]
▶ I was surprised to hear that.
私はそれを聞いて驚きました。
★ surprising は「(ものやことが)驚くべき」

0237
afraid
アふレイド
[əfréid]
入試

形 [怖がって, (I'm afraid ～ で)残念ながら～]
▶ I'm afraid you have the wrong number.
あいにくですが番号をお間違えだと思います。

0238
each
イーチ
[i:tʃ]
入試

形 [それぞれの]
▶ Each country has its own culture.
それぞれの国にはそれぞれの文化がある。
★ each other で「お互い」

0239 exciting
イクサイティング
[iksáitiŋ]
入試

形 [(人を) わくわくさせる]
► The game was exciting.
その試合はわくわくするものだった。
★ excited は「(人が) わくわくした」

0240 professional
プロふェショヌる
[prəféʃ(ə)n(ə)l]

形 [プロの, 専門職の]
► a professional baseball player
プロの野球選手

0241 wild
ワイるド
[waild]

形 [野生の]
► a wild bear 野生のクマ

0242 angry
アングリィ
[ǽŋgri]
入試

形 [怒っている]
► Why is he angry? なぜ彼は怒っているの?
★ get angry で「怒る」

0243 another
アナざァ
[ənʌ́ðər]
入試

形 [もう1つ[1人]の, 別の]
► another cup of tea もう1杯の紅茶
★ 後には数えられる名詞の単数形がくる

0244 delicious
ディリシャス
[dilíʃəs]
入試

形 [おいしい]
► This cake looks delicious.
このケーキはおいしそうだ。

0245 foreign
ふォ(ー)リン
[fɔ́(:)r(ə)n]
入試

形 [外国の]
► a foreign language 外国語
派 foreigner 名 外国人

0246 important
インポータント
[impɔ́:rt(ə)nt]
入試

形 [重要な]
► an important event 重要な行事
派 importance 名 重要性

another は an+other だから名詞の単数形があとに続くよ。

🎧 0247〜0262

0247
interesting
インタレスティング
[ínt(ə)rəstiŋ]
入試

形 [おもしろい，興味深い]
► an interesting story 興味深い話
★ be interested in ~で「~に興味がある」

0248
tired
タイアド
[taiərd]
入試

形 [飽きて ⟨of ~ ~に⟩]
► I'm sick and tired of exams.
試験にはうんざりしている。
★「~で疲れて」は tired from ~

0249
useful
ユースふる
[júːsf(ə)l]
入試

形 [役立つ]
► useful information 役立つ情報

0250
warm
ウォーム
[wɔːrm]
入試

形 [暖かい]
► I like warm weather. 暖かい天候が好きだ。
⇔ cool 涼しい

0251
hungry
ハングリィ
[hʌ́ŋgri]
入試

形 [空腹の]
► Are you hungry? お腹がすいていますか。
⇔ full 満腹で

0252
lost
ろ(ー)スト
[lɔ(ː)st]

形 [道に迷った]
► I was lost in the forest. 森で迷った。
★ get lost は「道に迷う」

0253
main
メイン
[mein]

形 [おもな]
► the main street 大通り
派 mainly 副 おもに

0254
native
ネイティヴ
[néitiv]

形 [原産の，ある土地生まれの]
► native birds その土地の鳥

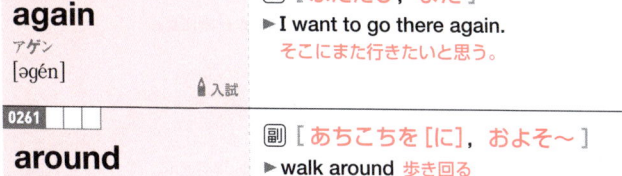

0255 nervous
ナ～ヴァス
[nə́ːrvəs]

形 [緊張した]
▶ I'm getting nervous. 緊張してきた。

0256 wrong
ロ(ー)ング
[rɔ(ː)ŋ]
入試

形 [間違った, (ものが)具合が悪い]
▶ take the wrong bus 間違ったバスに乗る

0257 first
ふァ～スト
[fəːrst]
入試

副 [最初に]
▶ do my homework first 最初に宿題をする
形 最初の
⇔ last 最後に, 最後の

0258 next
ネクスト
[nekst]
入試

副 [次に]
▶ what to do next 次に何をすべきか
形 次の

0259 also
オーるソウ
[ɔ́ːlsou]
入試

副 [～もまた]
▶ I also like cats. 私は猫も好きだ。
≒ too ～もまた

0260 again
アゲン
[əgén]
入試

副 [ふたたび, また]
▶ I want to go there again.
そこにまた行きたいと思う。

0261 around
アラウンド
[əráund]
入試

副 [あちこちを[に], およそ～]
▶ walk around 歩き回る
前 のあちこちを[に]

0262 before
ビふォー
[bifɔ́ːr]
入試

副 [以前に]
▶ I've been there before.
以前にそこへ行ったことがある。
前 の前に 接 ～する前に

このページからは副詞だよ。

0263 hard
ハード
[hɑːrd]
入試

副 [熱心に, 激しく]
► study very hard とても熱心に勉強する
形 大変な, つらい, 難しい

0264 just
ヂャスト
[dʒʌst]
入試

副 [たった今, ちょうど, ちょっと]
► I've just had lunch.
　たった今, 昼食をとったところだ。
★現在完了の文でよく使う

0265 often
オ(ー)フン
[ɔ́(ː)f(ə)n]
入試

副 [よく, しばしば]
► He often goes to the movies.
　彼はよく映画を見に行く。

0266 later
れイタァ
[léitər]
入試

副 [あとで]
► I'll call back later.
　あとで(電話を)かけ直します。

0267 yet
イェット
[jet]
入試

副 [(否定文で)まだ(〜ない), (疑問文で)もう]
► I haven't finished it yet.
　まだそれを終えていない。

0268 together
トゥゲざァ
[təɡéðər]
入試

副 [一緒に]
► play together 一緒に遊ぶ

0269 ago
アゴウ
[əɡóu]
入試

副 [〜前に]
► ten years ago 10年前に

0270 never
ネヴァ
[névər]
入試

副 [一度も〜ない, 決して〜ない]
► I've never seen a koala.
　一度もコアラを見たことがない。
★現在完了の否定文でよく使う

0271 ever
エヴァ [évər] 入試

副 [今までに]
► Have you ever tried tacos?
今までにタコスを食べたことはありますか。
★現在完了の疑問文でよく使う

0272 outside
アウトサイド [àutsáid] 入試

副 [外(側)に[で, へ]]
► play outside 戸外で遊ぶ
前 の外へ[に, で] 名 外(側)
⇔ inside (の)内(側)に[で, へ], 屋内に, 内(側)

0273 still
スティる [stíl] 入試

副 [今でも, まだ]
► It's still dark outside. 外はまだ暗い。

0274 tonight
トゥナイト [tənáit]

副 [今夜(は)]
► I'll call you tonight. 今夜君に電話するよ。
名 今夜

0275 already
オーるレディ [ɔ:lrédi] 入試

副 [すでに, もう]
► I've already finished my homework.
もう宿題は終えた。
★現在完了の肯定文でよく使う

0276 usually
ユージュ(ア)りィ [jú:ʒu(ə)li] 入試

副 [いつもは, たいてい]
► I usually get up at seven.
私はたいてい7時に起きる。
派 usual 形 いつもの, ふつうの

0277 early
ア〜りィ [ə́:rli] 入試

副 [早く]
► go home early 早く家に帰る
形 早い, 初期の
⇔ late 遅く, 遅い

0278 part-time
パートタイム [pà:rttáim]

副 [パートタイムで, 非常勤で]
► work part-time アルバイトをする
形 パートタイムの
⇔ full-time 常勤で, 常勤の

現在完了の文でよく使う副詞を確認しよう。

0279
even
イーヴン
[íːv(ə)n]
入試

副 [～でさえ，（比較級を強めて）さらに]
▶ He works hard, even on Sundays.
彼はよく働く。日曜でさえも。

0280
everywhere
エヴリ(フ)ウェア
[évri(h)weər]

副 [どこでも，いたるところに]
▶ take the camera everywhere
カメラをどこへでも持っていく

0281
far
ふァー
[fɑːr]
入試

副 [遠方に[へ]]
▶ The station is not far from here.
駅はここから遠くありません。

0282
once
ワンス
[wʌns]
入試

副 [一度，かつて]
▶ I've been here once.
ここへは一度来たことがある。
★現在完了の文でよく使う

0283
when
(フ)ウェン
[(h)wen]
入試

接 [～するとき]
▶ when I was ten 私が10歳だったときに
副 いつ

0284
if
イふ
[if]
入試

接 [もし～ならば]
▶ if it's sunny tomorrow 明日晴れたら
★ふつうは未来のことでも現在形で表す

0285
because
ビコ(ー)ズ
[bikɔ́(ː)z]
入試

接 [（なぜなら）～だから]
▶ because I was busy 忙しかったので
★後に〈主語〉+〈動詞〉の形で理由を続ける

0286
than
ざン
[ðæn]
入試

接 [～よりも]
▶ It's colder than yesterday. 昨日より寒い。
★比較級とともに使う

0287
until
アンティる
[əntíl]
入試

接 [〜するまで]
▶ play until it gets dark 暗くなるまで遊ぶ
前 〜まで

0288
while
(フ)ワイる
[(h)wail]
入試

接 [〜する間に]
▶ while I'm away 私の外出中に
名 (しばらくの)間
★during は前置詞で「〜の間(中)」

0289
by
バイ
[bai]
入試

前 [〜までに, のそばに, によって]
▶ Be back by nine. 9時までに戻りなさい。
★by「によって」は受身形の文でよく使う

0290
over
オウヴァ
[óuvər]
入試

前 [〜より多く, の上方に]
▶ over a hundred people 100人を超える人々
副 終わって
⇔ under の下に[を]

0291
between
ビトゥウィーン
[bitwíːn]
入試

前 [(2つのもの[人])の間に[で]]
▶ between classes 授業の合間に
★between A and B で「AとBの間に[で]」

0292
during
ドゥーリング
[dúːriŋ]
入試

前 [の間(中)]
▶ during lunch break 昼休みの間(中)
★while「〜する間に」は接続詞で, 後に(主語)＋(動詞)が続く

0293
since
スィンス
[sins]
入試

前 [〜以来]
▶ since this morning 今朝から
接 〜して以来
★現在完了の文で使う

0294
across
アクロ(ー)ス
[əkrɔ́(ː)s]
入試

前 [を横切って]
▶ swim across the river 川を泳いで渡る
★across from 〜で「〜の向かいに」

0295
one
ワン
[wʌn]
入試

代 [(1つの)もの, (1人の)人]
► The bigger one, please.
大きい方をください。
★one は前に出た数えられる1つのもの[人]を表す

0296
all
オール
[ɔːl]
入試

代 [すべてのもの[人]]
► All of the students were friendly.
生徒はみんな親切でした。
形 すべての

0297
anyone
エニワン
[éniwʌn]
入試

代 [(疑問文で)だれか, (否定文で)だれも(~ない)]
► Does anyone know? だれか知ってる?
★肯定文で「だれでも」

0298
should
シュッド
[ʃud]
入試

助 [~すべきだ, ~した方がよい]
► We should hurry. 急いだ方がいいね。

0299
could
クッド
[kud]
入試

助 [~することができた(can の過去形)]
► I couldn't meet him yesterday.
昨日は彼に会えなかった。

0300
must
マスト
[mʌst]
入試

助 [~しなければならない]
► I must go to the dentist.
歯医者に行かなければならない。
★must に過去形はなく, had to を使う

単語編 でる度 A
チェックテスト

1 下線の語句の意味を①〜③の中から選びましょう。

(1) <u>move</u> to the U.S.　①楽しむ　②学ぶ　③移り住む

(2) <u>save</u> money　①を貯える　②を費やす　③を与える

(3) <u>draw</u> a picture　①を選ぶ　②を描く　③を売る

(4) visit an <u>island</u>　①農場　②会社　③島

(5) We go to the <u>same</u> school.
　①異なった　②特別な　③同じ

2 下線の単語の意味を答えましょう。

(1) <u>return</u> a book to him　彼に本（　　　　　　　　）

(2) on the third <u>floor</u>　3（　　　　　　　　）に

(3) work at a <u>factory</u>　（　　　　　　　　）で働く

(4) We have <u>enough</u> time.
　私たちには（　　　　　　　　）時間がある。

これで「でる度A」は終わりだよ。がんばったね！

3 日本語に合うように（　）に英単語を入れましょう。

(1) 花を植える　　　　　　　　（　　　　　　）flowers

(2) 服を着替える　　　　　　　change（　　　　　　）

(3) ボランティアとして働く　　work as a（　　　　　　）

(4) 私はその知らせを聞いて驚いた。
　　I was（　　　　　　）to hear the news.

(5) 木を育てる　　　　　　　　（　　　　　　）trees

(6) 情報を得る　　　　　　　　get（　　　　　　）

(7) 休暇の間（中）　　　　　　（　　　　　　）the holidays

(8) 彼らはちょうど公園に着いたところだ。
　　They have（　　　　　　）arrived at the park.

4 下線の単語の反意語（⇔）とその意味を答えましょう。

(1) **lend** a book　⇔　（　　　　　　）a book
　　　　　　　　　　　　本（　　　　）

(2) my **husband**　⇔　my（　　　　　　）
　　　　　　　　　　　　私の（　　　　）

(3) get up **late**　⇔　get up（　　　　　　）
　　　　　　　　　　　　（　　　　）起きる

正解

1 (1) ③（⇒p.12）　(2) ①（⇒p.15）　(3) ②（⇒p.18）　(4) ③（⇒p.33）
(5) ③（⇒p.40）

2 (1) を返す（⇒p.15）　(2) 階（⇒p.29）　(3) 工場（⇒p.26）
(4) 十分な（⇒p.39）

3 (1) plant（⇒p.13）　(2) clothes（⇒p.32）　(3) volunteer（⇒p.22）
(4) surprised（⇒p.40）　(5) grow（⇒p.11）　(6) information（⇒p.21）
(7) during（⇒p.47）　(8) just（⇒p.44）

4 (1) borrow／を借りる（⇒p.16）　(2) wife／妻（⇒p.31）
(3) early／早く（⇒p.45）

でる度

B

単語編

よくでる重要単語 300

- 動詞 (60語) …………………… 52
- 名詞 (161語) ………………… 60
- 形容詞・副詞・その他 (79語) … 81
- チェックテスト ……………… 91

でる度 B は，よく出題される重要単語です。ここに掲載されている 300 語を覚えることで，3 級の合格がぐっと近付きます。

	1周目	2周目	3周目
動	/	/	/
名	/	/	/
形・副・他	/	/	/

でる度 B よくでる重要単語

動詞　60語

0301〜0315

0301
deliver
ディリヴァ
[dilívər]

[を運ぶ]
► deliver them to his house
　それらを彼の家に運ぶ

0302
answer
アンサァ
[ǽnsər]　入試

[(に)答える，(電話)(に)出る]
► answer the questions　質問に答える
图 答え，返事

0303
believe
ビリーヴ
[bilíːv]　入試

[(を)信じる]
► believe that he can win
　彼は勝てると信じる
★that節(that＋主語＋動詞)が続く動詞

0304
collect
コれクト
[kəlékt]　入試

[を集める]
► collect garbage　ごみを集める
派 collection 图 収集

0305
cost
コ(ー)スト
[kɔ(ː)st]

[(費用)がかかる]
► How much does it cost?
　それはいくらですか。
图 値段，費用　★[過去・過分] cost

0306
cross
クロ(ー)ス
[krɔ(ː)s]

[を横切る，渡る]
► cross the street　通りを横断する
★across「を横切って」は前置詞

0307
die
ダイ
[dai]　入試

[死ぬ]
► He died at the age of 90.
　彼は90歳でこの世を去った。
派 death 图 死，死亡　dead 形 死んでいる

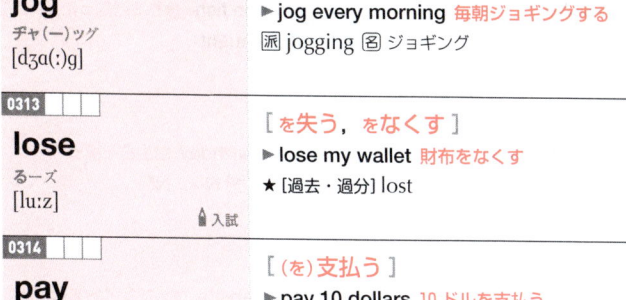

0308
enter
エンタァ
[éntər]

[(に)入る]
▶ enter the room 部屋に入る
≒ go into ~ ~に入る
派 entrance 名 入り口

0309
fall
ふォール
[fɔːl]　🔒入試

[落ちる]
▶ fall from a tree 木から落ちる
★「自転車から落ちる」は fall off a bike
★ [過去] fell　[過分] fallen

0310
fight
ふァイト
[fait]

[(と)戦う,けんかする]
▶ fight in a war 戦争で戦う
名 戦い,けんか
★ [過去・過分] fought

0311
hurt
ハ~ト
[həːrt]　🔒入試

[痛む,を傷つける]
▶ My leg hurts. 脚が痛い。
★ [過去・過分] hurt

0312
jog
ヂャ(ー)ッグ
[dʒɑ(ː)g]

[ジョギングする]
▶ jog every morning 毎朝ジョギングする
派 jogging 名 ジョギング

0313
lose
るーズ
[luːz]　🔒入試

[を失う,をなくす]
▶ lose my wallet 財布をなくす
★ [過去・過分] lost

0314
pay
ペイ
[pei]　🔒入試

[(を)支払う]
▶ pay 10 dollars 10ドルを支払う
★ [過去・過分] paid

0315
protect
プロテクト
[prətékt]　🔒入試

[を保護する]
▶ protect the environment
　自然環境を保護する

It costs a lot. = It is expensive. だよ。

0316 reach
リーチ
[riːtʃ]
入試

[に着く，に届く]
► reach the top of the mountain
山頂にたどり着く

0317 ride
ライド
[raid]
入試

[(に)乗る]
► ride a bike 自転車に乗る
★ give + (人) + a ride で「(人)を車で送る」
★ [過去] rode [過分] ridden

0318 share
シェア
[ʃeər]
入試

[を共有する，を分け合う]
► share opinions 意見を共有する

0319 agree
アグリー
[əgríː]
入試

[賛成する，同意する]
► I agree with you. あなたに賛成です。
⇔ disagree 反対する
★ agree with + (人) で「(人)に同意する」

0320 catch
キャッチ
[kætʃ]
入試

[を捕まえる]
► I caught three fish. 魚を3匹釣った。
★ [過去・過分] caught

0321 celebrate
セレブレイト
[séləbreit]

[を祝う]
► celebrate a birthday 誕生日を祝う
派 celebration 名 祝い，祝典

0322 check
チェック
[tʃek]

[を調べる]
► check the website ウェブサイトを調べる

0323 contact
カ(ー)ンタクト
[ká(ː)ntækt]

[に連絡をとる]
► contact Ann at 333-4567
333-4567番のアンに電話をする
★ contact to + (人) としない

0324
expect
イクスペクト
[ikspékt]

[を予期する，を期待する]
▶ expect a letter 手紙を期待して待つ

0325
fly
ふらイ
[flai] 　入試

[飛行機で行く，飛ぶ]
▶ I flew to China. 飛行機で中国へ飛んだ。
派 flight 名 飛行機の便，飛行
★ [過去] flew　[過分] flown

0326
follow
ふァ(ー)ろウ
[fá(:)lou] 　入試

[に従う，のあとについていく]
▶ follow the rule 規則に従う

0327
forget
ふォゲット
[fərgét] 　入試

[(を)忘れる]
▶ forget her name 彼女の名前を忘れる
⇔ remember (を)思い出す，(を)覚えている
★ [過去] forgot　[過分] forgotten, forgot

0328
hit
ヒット
[hit] 　入試

[(を)打つ]
▶ hit my head on a door ドアに頭をぶつける
★ [過去・過分] hit

0329
hurry
ハ〜リィ
[hə́:ri] 　入試

[急ぐ]
▶ Hurry up! 急いで！
名 急ぎ，急ぐ必要
★ be in a hurry で「急いでいる，あわてている」

0330
invent
インヴェント
[invént]

[を発明する]
▶ It was invented by Edison.
それはエジソンによって発明された。
派 invention 名 発明，発明品

0331
kill
キる
[kil] 　入試

[を殺す]
▶ My dog was killed in an accident.
私の犬は事故で死にました。

0332 pass
パス
[pæs] 入試

[に合格する,を手渡す]
▶ pass the exam 試験に合格する
⇔ fail (試験)に落ちる

0333 perform
パふォーム
[pərfɔ́:rm]

[を上演する,(を)演じる]
▶ The students performed a play.
学生たちが劇を上演した。
派 performance 名 公演,演技

0334 shut
シャット
[ʃʌt]

[を閉める,閉まる]
▶ shut the door ドアを閉める
≒ close を閉める,閉まる
★ [過去・過分] shut

0335 smell
スメる
[smel] 入試

[(形容詞の前で)のにおいがする]
▶ That smells nice. いいにおいだ。
名 におい

0336 taste
テイスト
[teist] 入試

[(形容詞の前で)の味がする]
▶ It tastes sweet. それは甘い味がする。
名 味
派 tasty 形 おいしい

0337 attack
アタック
[ətǽk]

[を攻撃する]
▶ The village was attacked by enemies.
その村は敵に攻撃されました。
名 攻撃

0338 carry
キャリィ
[kǽri] 入試

[を運ぶ]
▶ carry it on a truck それをトラックで運ぶ

0339 continue
コンティニュ(ー)
[kəntínju(:)] 入試

[続く,を続ける]
▶ continue until next year 来年まで続く
≒ last 続く
★ continue to do [doing] で「〜し続ける」

0340
cry
クライ
[krai]
入試

[泣く，叫ぶ]
▶ Don't cry. 泣かないで。

0341
destroy
ディストゥロイ
[distrói]

[を破壊する]
▶ Many houses were destroyed.
多くの家屋が破壊された。

0342
exchange
イクスチェインヂ
[ikstʃéindʒ]
入試

[を交換する]
▶ exchange e-mail addresses
Eメールアドレスを交換する
名 交換

0343
fit
ふィット
[fit]

[(サイズ，型が)に合う]
▶ It fits me perfectly. それは私にぴったりだ。
★「(色などが)に似合う」は suit
★[過去・過分] fitted, fit

0344
guess
ゲス
[ges]
入試

[(を)推測する]
▶ guess the meaning 意味を推測する

0345
imagine
イマヂン
[imædʒin]
入試

[を想像する]
▶ Can you imagine why?
なぜだか想像できますか。
派 image 名 イメージ，像

0346
introduce
イントゥロドゥース
[ìntrədúːs]
入試

[を紹介する]
▶ introduce him to my parents
両親に彼を紹介する
★introduce A to B でよく使う

0347
jump
ヂャンプ
[dʒʌmp]
入試

[跳ぶ]
▶ jump from a window 窓から飛び降りる

---

smell や taste は，look や sound のようにあとに形容詞が続くよ。

0348
mean
ミーン
[miːn]
入試

[を意味する]
► What does it mean? それは何という意味か。
派 meaning 名 意味
★ [過去・過分] meant

0349
order
オーダァ
[ɔ́ːrdər]
入試

[(を)注文する]
► Can we order? 注文してもいいですか。
名 注文

0350
push
プッシ
[puʃ]
入試

[(を)押す]
► push a button ボタンを押す
≒ press を押す
⇔ pull (を)引く

0351
relax
リらックス
[rilǽks]

[くつろぐ]
► go to the cafeteria to relax
くつろぎにカフェテリアへ行く

0352
sail
セイる
[seil]

[航海する]
► go sailing 航海に出る
名 帆, 帆船
派 sailor 名 船乗り

0353
serve
サ〜ヴ
[səːrv]

[(食べ物など)を出す]
► serve good wine よいワインを出す

0354
shake
シェイク
[ʃeik]

[を振る, (相手の手)を握る]
► shake hands 握手をする

0355
shout
シャウト
[ʃaut]
入試

[(と)叫ぶ, どなる]
► He shouted, "Wait for me!"
彼は「待って！」と叫んだ。

0356	snowboard スノウボード [snóubɔːrd]	[スノーボードをする] ► Can you snowboard? スノーボードはできますか。 名 スノーボード（の板）
0357	steal スティール [stiːl] 入試	[を盗む] ► My bike was stolen. 自転車が盗まれた。 ★ [過去] stole　[過分] stolen
0358	throw すロウ [θrou] 入試	[(を)投げる] ► throw a ball ボールを投げる ★ [過去] threw　[過分] thrown
0359	wake ウェイク [weik] 入試	[目が覚める ⟨up⟩] ► I woke up at six. 6時に目が覚めた。 ★ [過去] woke, waked　[過分] woken, waked
0360	welcome ウェるカム [wélkəm] 入試	[を歓迎する] ► He was welcomed by everyone. 彼はみんなから歓迎された。 形 歓迎される

でる度 Ⓑ よくでる重要単語

名詞　161語

🎧 0361〜0375

0361 height
ハイト
[hait]
[高さ，身長]
▶ What's the height of the tower?
その塔の高さはどれくらいですか。
派 high 形 高い

0362 hurricane
ハ〜リケイン
[hə́ːrəkein]
[ハリケーン]
▶ A hurricane hit the town.
ハリケーンがその町を襲った。
★「台風」は typhoon

0363 ice cream
アイス　クリーム
[áis kriːm]
[アイスクリーム]
▶ an ice cream shop　アイスクリーム店

0364 Olympic
オリンピック
[əlímpik]
[(the 〜s で)オリンピック]
▶ the 2012 London Olympics
2012年ロンドンオリンピック
★the Olympic Games とも言う

0365 parade
パレイド
[pəréid]
[パレード]
▶ take part in a parade　パレードに参加する

0366 stamp
スタンプ
[stæmp]
[切手]
▶ put a stamp on the postcard
はがきに切手をはる

0367 worker
ワ〜カァ
[wə́ːrkər]
[労働者，従業員]
▶ workers at the factory　その工場の労働者

0368 air
エア [eər]
[空気]
► fresh air 新鮮な空気

0369 airport
エアポート [éərpɔ̀:rt]
[空港]
► Could you take me to the airport?
私を空港に連れていってくださいませんか。

0370 bike
バイク [baik]
[自転車]
► go by bike 自転車で行く
= bicycle

0371 cafeteria
キャフェティ(ア)リア [kæfətí(ə)riə]
[カフェテリア, 食堂]
► have lunch at a cafeteria
カフェテリアで昼食をとる

0372 chance
チャンス [tʃæns]
[機会, 可能性]
► have a chance to go abroad
海外へ行く機会を持つ

0373 circle
サ〜クる [sə́:rkl]
[円]
► in a circle 輪になって

0374 customer
カスタマァ [kʌ́stəmər]
[(店などの)客]
► make customers angry 客を怒らせる

0375 dream
ドゥリーム [dri:m]
[(将来の)夢, (睡眠中に見る)夢]
► I hope my dream comes true.
夢がかなうといいな。

cafeteria は学校や会社などにある屋内の食堂のことだよ。

0376 ear
イア
[iər]

[耳]
► I can't believe my ears. 耳を疑う話だ。

0377 exam
イグザム
[igzǽm]

[試験]
► have an English exam 英語の試験がある
= examination

0378 fire
ふァイア
[fáiər]   入試

[火, (数えられる名詞で)火事]
► There was a fire yesterday.
昨日、火事があった。

0379 million
ミリョン
[míljən]

[100万]
► two million years ago 200万年前に
★billion で「10億」

0380 mountain
マウントゥン
[máunt(ə)n]   入試

[山]
► go to the mountains 山へ行く

0381 page
ペイヂ
[peidʒ]

[ページ]
► Answer the questions on page 8.
8ページの質問に答えなさい。

0382 panda
パンダ
[pǽndə]

[パンダ]
► pandas from China 中国から来たパンダ

0383 phone
ふォウン
[foun]   入試

[電話]
► answer the phone 電話に出る
= telephone

0384
photo
ふォウトウ
[fóutou]

[写真]
▶ a photo contest 写真コンクール
= photograph ≒ picture 絵, 写真
派 photographer 名 写真家

0385
poster
ポウスタァ
[póustər]

[ポスター]
▶ the poster on the wall
壁にはってあるポスター

0386
present
プレズント
[préz(ə)nt]
入試

[プレゼント]
▶ a birthday present 誕生日プレゼント
≒ gift 贈り物

0387
problem
プラ(ー)ブレム
[prá(:)bləm]
入試

[問題]
▶ have a problem with my grade
成績に問題がある

0388
race
レイス
[reis]
入試

[競走, レース]
▶ practice for the race
レースに向けて練習する

0389
rule
ルーる
[ru:l]

[規則, ルール]
▶ break a rule 規則を破る

0390
scarf
スカーふ
[skɑ:rf]

[スカーフ]
▶ wear a scarf around my neck
スカーフを首に巻く

0391
star
スター
[stɑ:r]
入試

[星, (テレビなどの)スター]
▶ bright stars in the night sky 夜空に輝く星
★ star は「恒星」で, 「惑星」は planet

0392
theater
すィアタァ
[θíətər]

[劇場，映画館]
▶ a movie theater 映画館

0393
uniform
ユーニふォーム
[júːnifɔːrm]

[ユニフォーム，制服]
▶ a school uniform 学生服

0394
wedding
ウェディング
[wédiŋ]

[結婚式]
▶ go to my cousin's wedding
いとこの結婚式に行く

0395
accident
アクスィデント
[æksid(ə)nt]

[事故]
▶ a car accident 自動車事故

0396
athlete
アすリート
[æθliːt]

[スポーツ選手]
▶ one of the best athletes
最も優れたスポーツ選手の1人

0397
bakery
ベイカリィ
[béik(ə)ri]

[パン屋]
▶ the bakery that opened last week
先週オープンしたパン屋

0398
bank
バンク
[bæŋk]

[銀行]
▶ Is there a bank around here?
この辺りに銀行はありますか。

0399
bicycle
バイスィクる
[báisikl]

[自転車]
▶ ride a bicycle 自転車に乗る
= bike

0400 captain
キャプトゥン
[kǽpt(ə)n]

[主将，船長]
▶ the captain of the soccer team
サッカーチームの主将

0401 celebration
セレブレイション
[sèləbréiʃ(ə)n]

[祝い，祝典]
▶ hold a celebration 祝賀会を開く
派 celebrate 動 を祝う

0402 cell phone
セるフォウン
[sél foun]

[携帯電話]
▶ Turn off your cell phone.
携帯電話の電源を切ってください。
= mobile phone

0403 center
センタァ
[séntər]   入試

[中心(地)，センター]
▶ a shopping center ショッピングセンター
派 central 形 中央の

0404 century
センチュリィ
[séntʃ(ə)ri]   入試

[世紀]
▶ in the 18th century 18世紀に

0405 child
チャイるド
[tʃáild]   入試

[子ども]
▶ when I was a child 私が子どもだったときに
≒ kid 子ども ⇔ adult 大人
★ [複数形] children

0406 Chinese
チャイニーズ
[tʃàiníːz]

[中国語，中国人]
▶ My sister studies Chinese.
妹は中国語を勉強しています。
形 中国(語[人])の

0407 cloth
クろ(ー)す
[klɔ(ː)θ]

[布]
▶ a piece of cloth 1枚の布
★ clothes は「衣服」

cloth や clothes, close (動・形) の発音も確認しよう。

0408 coat
コウト
[kout]

[(衣服の)コート]
► Take your coat with you.
コートを持っていきなさい。

0409 dollar
ダ(ー)らァ
[dá(:)lər] 入試

[ドル]
► All the CDs are just 8 dollars!
全CDがたったの8ドルです！

0410 dress
ドゥレス
[dres] 入試

[ドレス]
► a girl in a dress ドレスを着た女の子

0411 example
イグザンプる
[igzǽmpl] 入試

[例，実例]
► Give me an example.
例を挙げてください。

0412 experience
イクスピ(ア)リエンス
[ikspí(ə)riəns] 入試

[経験]
► have a good experience よい経験をする

0413 fence
ふェンス
[fens]

[囲い，さく]
► build a fence 囲いを作る

0414 German
ヂャ〜マン
[dʒə́:rmən]

[ドイツ語，ドイツ人]
► take a German class
ドイツ語の授業を履修する
形 ドイツ(語[人])の 派 Germany 图 ドイツ

0415 grade
グレイド
[greid]

[成績]
► get the best grade in the class
クラスでいちばんよい成績を取る

0416 grandfather
グラン(ド)ふァーざァ
[grǽn(d)fàːðər]

[祖父]
► go fishing with my grandfather
　祖父と釣りに行く
= grandpa ⇔ grandmother 祖母

0417 hamburger
ハンバ〜ガァ
[hǽmbəːrgər]

[ハンバーガー]
► a hamburger shop　ハンバーガーショップ

0418 hometown
ホウムタウン
[hòumtáun]

[故郷, 住み慣れた町]
► miss my hometown　故郷が恋しい

0419 Internet
インタァネット
[íntərnet]　入試

[インターネット]
► buy clothes on the Internet
　インターネットで衣服を買う

0420 line
らイン
[lain]　入試

[列, 線]
► wait in a long line　長い列に並んで待つ

0421 living room
りヴィング ルーム
[lívɪŋ ruːm]

[居間]
► relax in the living room　居間でくつろぐ
★ living は「生活(の)」

0422 locker
ら(ー)カァ
[lá(ː)kər]

[ロッカー]
► rest in the locker room
　ロッカールームで休む

0423 manager
マネヂャ
[mǽnidʒər]

[支配人]
► talk to the shop manager　店長と話す

0424
meal
ミール
[miːl]

[食事]
▶ after each meal 毎食後に

0425
museum
ミュ(ー)ズィ(ー)アム
[mjuː(ː)zíː(ː)əm]   入試

[博物館，美術館]
▶ an art museum 美術館

0426
point
ポイント
[pɔint]   入試

[点]
▶ score three points 3点取る
動 指さす

0427
pollution
ポるーション
[pəlúːʃ(ə)n]

[汚染]
▶ pollution in the river 川の汚染
派 pollute 動 を汚染する

0428
reason
リーズン
[ríːz(ə)n]   入試

[理由]
▶ explain the reason for being late
遅れた理由を説明する

0429
recipe
レスィピ
[résəpi]

[調理法，レシピ]
▶ Can you tell me the recipe?
そのレシピを教えてくれる？

0430
sale
セイる
[seil]

[特売，セール]
▶ a special sale 特別セール

0431
sandwich
サン(ド)ウィッチ
[sǽn(d)witʃ]

[サンドイッチ]
▶ order tuna sandwiches
ツナサンドを注文する

0432 science
サイエンス [sáiəns] 入試

[理科，科学]
▶ science homework 理科の宿題
派 scientist 名 科学者

0433 secret
スィークレット [síːkrət] 入試

[秘密]
▶ the secret between us
私たち２人だけの秘密
形 秘密の

0434 side
サイド [said] 入試

[側，側面]
▶ on the right side 右側に

0435 slice
スライス [slais]

[(薄切りの)１切れ]
▶ a slice of bread パン１枚

0436 textbook
テクストブック [tékstbuk]

[教科書]
▶ Open your textbooks. 教科書を開きなさい。

0437 tool
トゥーる [tuːl]

[道具]
▶ use a special tool 特別な道具を使う

0438 top
タ(ー)ップ [tɑ(ː)p] 入試

[頂上，上部]
▶ the top of the mountain 山の頂上
⇔ bottom 底

0439 tour
トゥア [tuər]

[周遊，ツアー]
▶ take a tour of Europe
ヨーロッパを周遊する

meal は lunch や dinner のような１回の食事のことだよ。

0440
tourist
トゥリスト
[túrəst]

[旅行客]
► welcome tourists 旅行客を歓迎する

0441
wood
ウッド
[wud]
🔒 入試

[木材]
► a chair made of wood 木でできたいす
★ woods で「森」の意味。tree は「樹木」

0442
actress
アクトゥレス
[ǽktrəs]

[女優]
► my favorite actress 私のお気に入りの女優
派 actor 名 俳優　act 動 (を)演じる, 行動する

0443
adventure
アドヴェンチャ
[ədvéntʃər]

[冒険]
► an adventure story 冒険物語
派 adventurer 名 冒険家

0444
alarm
アらーム
[əlá:rm]

[警報, アラーム]
► an alarm clock 目覚まし時計

0445
barbecue
バーベキュー
[bá:rbikju:]

[バーベキュー]
► enjoy barbecue lunch
　バーベキューランチを楽しむ

0446
bathroom
バすルーム
[bǽθru:m]

[浴室, トイレ]
► go to the bathroom トイレに行く
★「浴槽」は bathtub

0447
beginner
ビギナァ
[bigínər]

[初心者]
► lessons for beginners
　初心者向けのレッスン

0448
bottom
バ(ー)トム
[bá(:)təm]

[底]
▶ on the bottom of the sea 海の底で
⇔ top 頂上, 上部

0449
bridge
ブリッヂ
[brɪdʒ] 入試

[橋]
▶ cross the bridge 橋を渡る

0450
coach
コウチ
[koutʃ]

[コーチ, 指導者]
▶ a tennis coach テニスコーチ

0451
comedy
カ(ー)メディ
[ká(:)mədi]

[喜劇, コメディー]
▶ watch a comedy on TV
テレビでコメディーを見る

0452
computer
コンピュータァ
[kəmpjú:tər] 入試

[コンピューター]
▶ use a computer コンピューターを使う

0453
continent
カ(ー)ンティネント
[ká(:)ntənənt]

[大陸]
▶ the European Continent ヨーロッパ大陸

0454
course
コース
[kɔːrs] 入試

[講座, 進路]
▶ take a cooking course
料理の講座を受講する

0455
court
コート
[kɔːrt]

[(テニスなどの)コート]
▶ a tennis court テニスコート

0456
decoration
デコレイション
[dèkəréiʃ(ə)n]

[飾り，装飾]
► Christmas decorations クリスマスの飾り
派 decorate 動 を飾る，を装飾する

0457
dentist
デンティスト
[déntist]

[歯医者，歯科医]
► go to the dentist 歯医者に行く

0458
description
ディスクリプション
[diskrípʃ(ə)n]

[描写，説明]
► the description of the bag I lost
私がなくしたかばんの説明
派 describe 動 を描写する，を説明する

0459
dessert
ディザ〜ト
[dizə́:rt]

[デザート]
► have ice cream for dessert
デザートにアイスクリームを食べる

0460
dining
ダイニング
[dáiniŋ]

[食事]
► a dining room 食堂，ダイニングルーム

0461
discount
ディスカウント
[dískaunt]

[割引]
► special discounts 特別割引

0462
doughnut
ドウナット
[dóunʌt]

[ドーナツ]
► a chocolate doughnut
チョコレートドーナツ

0463
entrance
エントゥランス
[éntr(ə)ns]

[入り口]
► meet at the entrance 入り口で会う
⇔ exit 出口
派 enter 動 (に)入る

0464 environment
インヴァイ(ア)ロンメント
[invái(ə)rənmənt] 入試

[環境]
► good for the environment 自然環境によい

0465 fact
ふアクト
[fækt] 入試

[事実]
► in fact 実は，それどころかむしろ

0466 fruit
ふルート
[fru:t] 入試

[果物]
► fruit salad フルーツサラダ
★ fruits salad ではないので注意

0467 gate
ゲイト
[geit] 入試

[門]
► a school gate 校門

0468 gift
ギふト
[gift]

[贈り物]
► wrap the gift 贈り物を包む
≒ present プレゼント

0469 goal
ゴウる
[goul]

[(サッカーなどの)ゴール，目標]
► get a goal 得点を入れる

0470 goldfish
ゴウるドふィッシ
[góuldfiʃ]

[金魚]
► feed my goldfish 金魚にえさをやる

0471 headache
ヘデイク
[hédeik]

[頭痛]
► I have a headache. 頭痛がします。
★ 胃痛[腹痛]は stomachache

entrance exam は「入り口の試験＝入学試験」だね。

0472
health
へるす
[helθ]
🔒入試

[健康]
▶ good for health 健康によい
派 healthy 形 健康的な

0473
hill
ヒる
[hil]
🔒入試

[丘, (低い)山]
▶ a house standing on a hill 丘の上に立つ家
★「(高い)山」は mountain

0474
hobby
ハ(ー)ビィ
[há(:)bi]

[趣味]
▶ Do you have any hobbies?
趣味はありますか。

0475
homestay
ホウムステイ
[hóumstei]

[ホームステイ]
▶ experience homestay in the U.S.
アメリカ合衆国でホームステイを経験する

0476
jeans
ヂーンズ
[dʒi:nz]

[(複数形で)ジーンズ]
▶ buy two pairs of jeans ジーンズを2本買う

0477
key
キー
[ki:]

[かぎ]
▶ the key to open the door
そのドアを開けるためのかぎ

0478
kid
キッド
[kid]

[子ども]
▶ pick up the kids 子どもたちを迎えにいく
≒ child 子ども

0479
kilogram
キろグラム
[kíləgræm]

[キログラム]
▶ five kilograms of rice 5キログラムの米
★ kilo は通常 kilometer ではなく kilogram の略

0480 kitchen
キチン [kítʃ(ə)n] 🔒入試

[台所]
► cook in the kitchen 台所で料理をする

0481 land
ランド [lænd] 🔒入試

[陸, 土地]
► the biggest animal living on land 陸上に住む最も大きな動物
動 着陸する

0482 language
ラングウェッヂ [læŋgwidʒ] 🔒入試

[言語]
► learn another language ほかの言語を学ぶ

0483 law
ろー [lɔː]

[法律]
► against the law 法律に反して
派 lawyer 名 弁護士

0484 librarian
らイブレ(ア)リアン [laibré(ə)riən]

[図書館員]
► ask the librarian at the counter カウンターの図書館員にたずねる
派 library 名 図書館

0485 mark
マーク [mɑːrk] 🔒入試

[印, しみ]
► a mark on the shirt シャツに付いたしみ

0486 mayor
メイア [méiər]

[市長]
► interview the mayor 市長にインタビューをする

0487 meat
ミート [miːt] 🔒入試

[肉]
► like meat better than fish 魚よりも肉を好む

0488
medal
メドゥる
[méd(ə)l]

[メダル]
▶ a gold medal 金メダル

0489
necklace
ネクれス
[nékləs]

[ネックレス]
▶ wear a necklace ネックレスを身につける

0490
nurse
ナ〜ス
[nəːrs]

[看護師]
▶ want to be a nurse 看護師になりたい
★「医師」は doctor

0491
painting
ペインティング
[péintiŋ]

[絵, 絵を描くこと]
▶ paintings at the museum 美術館の絵
派 paint 動 にペンキを塗る, を絵の具で描く

0492
pancake
パンケイク
[pǽnkeik]

[パンケーキ]
▶ make pancakes パンケーキを作る

0493
price
プライス
[prais]

[価格]
▶ at a low price 安い価格で
★価格が「高い」は high, 「低い」は low

0494
project
プラ(ー)ヂェクト
[prá(ː)dʒekt]

[計画, 事業]
▶ a space project 宇宙計画

0495
promise
プラ(ー)ミス
[prá(ː)məs]

入試

[約束]
▶ break a promise 約束を破る
動 (を [に]) 約束する

0496
queen
クウィーン
[kwi:n]

[女王]
▶ the Queen of England イングランドの女王
⇔ king 王

0497
rest
レスト
[rest]

[休息]
▶ the rest area 休憩場所
動 休息する

0498
rock
ラ(ー)ック
[rɑ(:)k]
入試

[ロック(音楽)，岩]
▶ sing in a rock band ロックバンドで歌う

0499
schoolwork
スクーるワ〜ク
[skúːlwəːrk]

[学校の勉強]
▶ have a lot of schoolwork
学校の課題がたくさんある

0500
science fiction
サイエンス ふィクション
[sàiəns fíkʃ(ə)n]

[空想科学小説，SF]
▶ science fiction movies SF映画

0501
section
セクション
[sékʃ(ə)n]

[区域，部門]
▶ look for the fish section 魚売り場を探す

0502
sentence
センテンス
[sént(ə)ns]

[文]
▶ write sentences with new words
新しく習った単語で文を書く

0503
sign
サイン
[sain]
入試

[看板，掲示]
▶ a shop with a big sign 大きな看板のある店
動 に署名する

名詞「署名」は signature と言うよ。

0504 **sir** サ〜 [sə:r]	[（男性に対して）お客様，先生] ▶ Certainly, sir. 承知しました，お客様。 ⇔ ma'am（女性に対して）お客様，先生 ★ 尊敬を込めた呼びかけ
0505 **snack** スナック [snæk]	[軽い食事，おやつ] ▶ buy snacks at the cafeteria カフェテリアで軽食を買う
0506 **stew** ストゥー [stu:]	[シチュー] ▶ beef stew ビーフシチュー
0507 **sweater** スウェタァ [swétər]	[セーター] ▶ a warm sweater 暖かいセーター
0508 **system** スィステム [sístəm]	[制度，体制] ▶ the school system 学校制度
0509 **telephone** テレフォウン [téləfoun] 入試	[電話] ▶ a telephone number 電話番号 = phone
0510 **thousand** さウザンド [θáuz(ə)nd] 入試	[1000] ▶ sixteen thousand people 1万6千人の人
0511 **trick** トゥリック [trik]	[芸当，いたずら] ▶ teach a dog tricks 犬に芸を教える

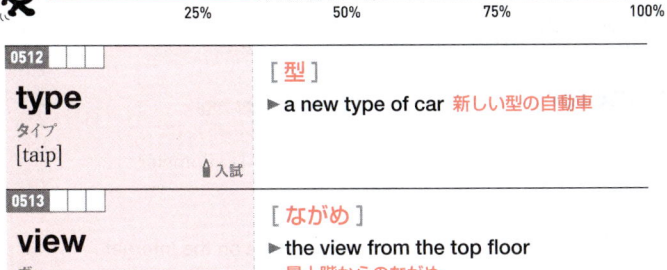

0512
type
タイプ
[taip]
入試

[型]
▶ a new type of car 新しい型の自動車

0513
view
ヴュー
[vju:]

[ながめ]
▶ the view from the top floor
最上階からのながめ

0514
village
ヴィれッヂ
[vílidʒ]
入試

[村]
▶ The girl was born in a small village.
その少女は小さな村で生まれた。

0515
waiter
ウェイタァ
[wéitər]

[ウエーター]
▶ a waiter in a restaurant
レストランのウエーター
⇔ waitress ウエートレス

0516
wallet
ワ(ー)れット
[wá(:)lət]

[財布]
▶ leave my wallet at home
財布を家に置き忘れる

0517
bottle
バ(ー)トゥる
[bá(:)tl]
入試

[びん]
▶ three bottles of wine 3本のワイン

0518
classmate
クらスメイト
[klǽsmeit]
入試

[同級生, クラスメート]
▶ with my classmates 同級生と一緒に

0519
classroom
クらスルーム
[klǽsru:m]
入試

[教室]
▶ clean the classroom 教室を掃除する

0520
meter
ミータァ
[míːtər]

[メートル]
▶ It's ten meters high.
それは高さ 10 メートルです。
★「キロメートル」は kilometer

0521
video
ヴィディオウ
[vídiou]
🔒 入試

[ビデオ]
▶ watch videos on the Internet
インターネットでビデオを見る

でる度 B よくでる重要単語

形容詞・副詞・その他 79語

0522 ～ 0528

0522
national
ナショヌる
[nǽʃ(ə)n(ə)l]

形 [国民の，国家の]
▶ a national park 国立公園

0523
crowded
クラウディッド
[kráudid]

形 [混雑した]
▶ The restaurant was crowded.
レストランは混んでいた。

0524
daily
デイりィ
[déili]

形 [毎日の，日常の]
▶ daily life 日常生活
≒ everyday 毎日の，日常の

0525
excited
イクサイティッド
[iksáitid] 入試

形 [(人が)わくわくした]
▶ He's excited. 彼はわくわくしている。
★ exciting は「(人を)わくわくさせる」，get excited で「わくわくする」

0526
female
ふィーメイる
[fí:meil]

形 [女性の]
▶ a female name 女性の名前
名 女性
⇔ male 男性の，男性

0527
junior
ヂューニャ
[dʒú:njər]

形 [年下の，下級の]
▶ a junior high school 中学校
★「高校」は (senior) high school

0528
loud
らウド
[laud]

形 [(声・音が)大きい]
▶ in a loud voice 大きな声で
⇔ quiet 静かな

meter の me の発音が「メー」でないことに注意しよう。

0529 male
メイる [meil]
形 [男性の]
▶ a male tiger オスのトラ
名 男性
⇔ female 女性の, 女性

0530 possible
パ(ー)スィブる [pá(:)səbl]
形 [可能な]
▶ as soon as possible 可能な限り早く
⇔ impossible 不可能な

0531 sad
サッド [sæd] 入試
形 [悲しい]
▶ feel sad 悲しむ
⇔ happy, glad うれしい
派 sadness 名 悲しみ

0532 such
サッチ [sʌtʃ] 入試
形 [そのような, このような]
▶ Where did you get such beautiful flowers? そんな美しい花をどこで買ったのですか。
★such (a [an]) + (形容詞) + (名詞)でよく使う

0533 easy
イーズィ [í:zi] 入試
形 [簡単な]
▶ an easy question 簡単な質問
⇔ difficult, hard 難しい
派 easily 副 簡単に, 容易に

0534 expensive
イクスペンスィヴ [ikspénsiv] 入試
形 [高価な]
▶ an expensive car 高価な車
⇔ cheap 安い, 安っぽい

0535 fast
ふァスト [fæst] 入試
形 [速い]
▶ a fast runner 足の速い走者
副 速く
⇔ slow 遅い

0536 few
ふュー [fju:] 入試
形 [(a few ~で)2,3の~, (few ~で)ほとんど~ない]
▶ a few days later 2,3日後に
★数えられない名詞には little を使う

0537 full
ふる
[ful]
入試

形 [いっぱいの，満腹で]
▶ I'm full. 満腹です。
⇔ hungry 空腹の

0538 half
ハフ
[hæf]
入試

形 [半分の]
▶ half an hour 30分
★「1時間半」は an hour and a half または one and a half hours

0539 heavy
ヘヴィ
[hévi]
入試

形 [重い，激しい]
▶ a heavy bag 重いかばん
⇔ light 軽い
派 heavily 副 重く，激しく

0540 homesick
ホウムスィック
[hóumsik]

形 [ホームシックの]
▶ She is homesick. 彼女はホームシックだ。
★ home (故郷) + sick (病気の)

0541 own
オウン
[oun]
入試

形 [自分自身の]
▶ our own country 私たち自身の国
動 を所有する
派 owner 名 所有者

0542 shy
シャイ
[ʃai]

形 [内気な]
▶ Don't be shy. 恥ずかしがらないで。

0543 silent
サイレント
[sáilənt]

形 [静かな，無音の]
▶ He was silent. 彼は黙っていた。
派 silence 名 静けさ，沈黙

0544 true
トゥルー
[tru:]
入試

形 [本当の]
▶ That's true. それは本当だ。
派 truth 名 真実

0545
wonderful
ワンダふる
[wʌ́ndərf(ə)l] 入試

形 [すばらしい]
▶ a wonderful experience すばらしい経験

0546
absent
アブセント
[ǽbs(ə)nt]

形 [(学校などを)欠席して ⟨from ~⟩]
▶ Nick has been absent from school for a week. ニックは1週間学校を欠席している。

0547
boring
ボーリング
[bɔ́ːriŋ]

形 [退屈な]
▶ a boring speech 退屈なスピーチ
★ bored は「(人が)退屈した」

0548
broken
ブロウクン
[bróuk(ə)n]

形 [壊れた]
▶ This computer is broken.
このコンピューターは壊れている。

0549
cheap
チープ
[tʃiːp]

形 [安い，安っぽい]
▶ the cheapest seat 最も安い座席
⇔ expensive 高価な

0550
cloudy
クらウディ
[kláudi]

形 [曇った]
▶ It's cloudy. 曇っている。
派 cloud 名 雲

0551
dangerous
デインヂャラス
[déindʒ(ə)rəs] 入試

形 [危険な]
▶ a dangerous job 危険な仕事
⇔ safe 安全な
派 danger 名 危険

0552
deep
ディープ
[diːp]

形 [深い]
▶ a deep lake 深い湖

0553 elementary
エレメンタリィ [èlimént(ə)ri]

形 [初級の]
► an elementary school 小学校

0554 enjoyable
インヂョイアブる [indʒɔ́iəbl]

形 [楽しい]
► sound enjoyable 楽しそうに聞こえる
派 enjoy 動 を楽しむ

0555 familiar
ふァミリャ [fəmíljər]

形 [見慣れた, 聞き慣れた]
► The name is familiar. その名前は聞き覚えがある。

0556 fresh
ふレッシ [freʃ]

形 [新鮮な]
► fresh fruit 新鮮な果物

0557 funny
ふァニィ [fʌ́ni]

形 [おかしい, こっけいな]
► a funny story こっけいな話

0558 human
ヒューマン [hjúːmən] 入試

形 [人間の, 人類の]
► the human body 人体
★ human being で「人, 人間」

0559 less
れス [les] 入試

形 [(little の比較級) より少ない]
► I have less free time than before. 私には以前ほど自由な時間がない。
副 より少なく

0560 narrow
ナロウ [nǽrou]

形 [(幅が) 狭い]
► Chile is a narrow country. チリは (幅が) 狭い国だ。
⇔ wide (幅が) 広い

「幅が狭い」は narrow, 「面積が小さい」は small だよ。

0561
perfect
パ〜フェクト
[pə́ːrfikt]

形 [完全な]
▶ a perfect performance 完ぺきな演技
派 perfectly 副 完全に

0562
poor
プァ
[puər]
入試

形 [貧しい，へたな，かわいそうな]
▶ poor children 貧しい子どもたち
⇔ rich 金持ちの

0563
public
パブリック
[pʌ́blik]

形 [公の]
▶ in public places 公共の場で

0564
smart
スマート
[smɑːrt]

形 [利口な]
▶ Jane is smart. ジェーンは利口だ。
★「体型がほっそりした，スマートな」は slim

0565
usual
ユージュ(ア)る
[júːʒu(ə)l]

形 [いつもの，ふつうの]
▶ earlier than usual いつもより早く
派 usually 副 いつもは，たいてい

0566
wide
ワイド
[waid]

形 [(幅が)広い]
▶ a wide river 幅が広い川
⇔ narrow (幅が)狭い

0567
short
ショート
[ʃɔːrt]
入試

形 [短い，背の低い]
▶ a girl with short hair 髪の短い女の子
⇔ tall 背の高い

0568
sunny
サニィ
[sʌ́ni]
入試

形 [晴れた]
▶ It was sunny this morning.
今朝は晴れていた。

0569 alone
アろウン
[əlóun]
入試

副 [1人で]
▶ live alone ひとり暮らしをしている

0570 anymore
エニモー
[ènimɔ́ːr]
入試

副 [(否定文で)これ以上(〜ない)]
▶ I don't need the book anymore.
　その本はもう必要ない。

0571 else
エるス
[els]
入試

副 [そのほかに]
▶ Do you need anything else?
　ほかに何か必要ですか。

0572 finally
ふァイナリィ
[fáin(ə)li]
入試

副 [ついに, 最後に]
▶ Finally, he found it under the desk.
　ついに, 彼は机の下にそれを見つけた。

0573 maybe
メイビ(ー)
[méibi(ː)]
入試

副 [もしかすると, たぶん]
▶ Maybe Mike has the key.
　マイクがかぎを持っているかもしれない。

0574 almost
オールモウスト
[ɔ́ːlmoust]
入試

副 [ほとんど]
▶ It's almost ready.
　その用意はほぼできている。

0575 easily
イーズィりィ
[íːzili]
入試

副 [簡単に, 容易に]
▶ You can find the building easily.
　その建物は簡単に見つかるよ。
派 easy 形 簡単な

0576 either
イーざァ
[íːðər]
入試

副 [(否定文で)〜もまた(…ない)]
▶ I don't like this food, either.
　私もこの食べ物が好きではない。
★この例文は肯定文なら I like this food, too.

0577 especially
イスペシャリィ [ispéʃ(ə)li]

副 [特に]
▶ He likes Japanese food, especially sushi. 彼は日本食，特にすしが好きだ。

0578 inside
インサイド [ìnsáid] 入試

副 [内(側)に [で，へ]，屋内に]
▶ Let's go inside. 中へ入ろう。
前 の中へ [に，で] 名 内(側)
⇔ outside (の)外(側)に [で，へ]，外(側)

0579 pretty
プリティ [príti] 入試

副 [とても，かなり]
▶ I'm pretty well, thanks.
とても元気です，ありがとう。
形 きれいな，かわいらしい

0580 sincerely
スィンスィアリィ [sinsíərli]

副 [(手紙の結びで)敬具]
▶ Sincerely, Lisa 敬具，リサより

0581 sometimes
サムタイムズ [sʌ́mtaimz] 入試

副 [ときどき]
▶ I sometimes meet him.
私はときどき彼に会う。

0582 twice
トゥワイス [twais]

副 [2度]
▶ I've visited Korea twice.
私は2度韓国を訪れたことがある。
★ two times とも言う。「1度」は once

0583 abroad
アブロード [əbrɔ́ːd]

副 [海外へ [で]]
▶ study abroad 海外留学する
≒ overseas 海外へ [で]

0584 ahead
アヘッド [əhéd]

副 [前方に 〈of ~ ~の〉]
▶ She was running ahead of me.
彼女は私の前を走っていた。

0585
cheaply
チープリィ
[tʃíːpli]

副 [安く]
► get the ticket more cheaply
チケットをより安く入手する
派 cheap 形 安い，安っぽい

0586
luckily
らキリィ
[lʌ́kili]

副 [幸運にも]
► Luckily, no one was injured.
幸運にも，だれもけがをしなかった。
派 lucky 形 運のよい

0587
someday
サムデイ
[sʌ́mdei]

副 [(未来の)いつか]
► I want to go to Paris someday.
いつかパリへ行きたい。
≒ sometime いつか

0588
straight
ストゥレイト
[streit]

副 [まっすぐに]
► go straight down the street
通りをまっすぐに行く
形 まっすぐな

0589
suddenly
サドゥンりィ
[sʌ́d(ə)nli]

副 [突然に]
► Suddenly, it started to rain.
突然，雨が降り出した。

0590
along
アろ(ー)ング
[əlɔ́(ː)ŋ]

前 [に沿って]
► walk along the street
通り沿いに歩く
★ across は「を横切って」

0591
beside
ビサイド
[bisáid]

前 [のそばに，の横に]
► stand beside him 彼の横に立つ
≒ next to ~　~の隣に

0592
against
アゲンスト
[əgénst]

前 [に対して，に反対して]
► the game against the Giants
ジャイアンツとの対戦
⇔ for に賛成して

luckily や suddenly などの文頭にくる副詞を確認しよう。

0593 behind
ビハインド [biháind] 入試

前 [の後ろに]
► sit behind him 彼の後ろに座る
⇔ in front of ～ ～の前で[に]

0594 without
ウィざウト [wiðáut] 入試

前 [～なしで，を持たずに]
► without his help 彼の手助けなしで
⇔ with があって，を持って
★without +（動詞の -ing 形）で「～せずに」

0595 anything
エニすィング [éniθiŋ] 入試

代 [（疑問文で）何か，（否定文で）何も（～ない）]
► Would you like anything else?
何かほかに必要ですか。

0596 both
ボウす [bouθ] 入試

代 [（2者について）両方とも]
► Both of them are soccer fans.
彼らは2人ともサッカーファンだ。
★both A and B で「A も B も（両方）」（副詞）

0597 something
サムすィング [sʌ́mθiŋ] 入試

代 [何か]
► something hot to drink 何か温かい飲み物

0598 herself
ハ～セるふ [hə:rsélf] 入試

代 [彼女自身を[に]]
► She made lunch by herself.
彼女は自分で昼食を作った。
★ほかに myself, yourself, himself などがある

0599 nothing
ナッすィング [nʌ́θiŋ] 入試

代 [何も～ない]
► have nothing special to do
特にすることがない

0600 someone
サムワン [sʌ́mwʌn] 入試

代 [だれか]
► someone who speaks French
だれかフランス語を話す人

単語編 でる度 B
チェックテスト

1 下線の語句の意味を①〜③の中から選びましょう。

(1) <u>**collect**</u> stamps ① を交換する ② をなくす ③ を集める
(2) <u>**follow**</u> the rule ① を忘れる ② に従う ③ を調べる
(3) a new <u>**project**</u> ① 問題 ② 法律 ③ 計画
(4) a beautiful <u>**view**</u> ① 山 ② ながめ ③ 絵
(5) It is <u>**dangerous**</u> to swim in the lake.
　① 簡単な ② 楽しい ③ 危険な

2 下線の単語の意味を答えましょう。

(1) <u>**protect**</u> the environment　自然環境（　　　　　　）
(2) a useful <u>**tool**</u>　　　　　　　役立つ（　　　　　）
(3) <u>**pollution**</u> in the river　　　川の（　　　　）
(4) My bike <u>**was stolen**</u>.　　　　自転車が（　　　　　　）。
(5) I <u>**introduced**</u> him to my parents.
　私は両親に彼（　　　　　　）。

これで「でる度B」は終わり。いよいよ「でる度C」だ！

3 日本語に合うように( )に英単語を入れましょう。

(1) 200万人　　　　　　　　two ( ) people

(2) 退屈な映画　　　　　　a ( ) movie

(3) それは甘い味がする。　It ( ) sweet.

(4) 私はいつもより早く寝た。
I went to bed earlier than ( ).

(5) 通りを横断する　　　　( ) the street

(6) 飛行機で中国へ飛ぶ　　( ) to China

(7) すばらしい経験をする　have a great ( )

4 下線の単語の反意語(⇔)とその意味を答えましょう。

(1) a <u>narrow</u> space　⇔　a ( ) space
　　　　　　　　　　　　　( )空間

(2) a <u>cheap</u> car　　⇔　an ( ) car
　　　　　　　　　　　　　( )車

(3) <u>remember</u> the telephone number
⇔　( ) the telephone number
電話番号( )

正解

1 (1) ③ (⇒p.52)　(2) ② (⇒p.55)　(3) ③ (⇒p.76)　(4) ② (⇒p.79)
(5) ③ (⇒p.84)

2 (1) を保護する (⇒p.53)　(2) 道具 (⇒p.69)　(3) 汚染 (⇒p.68)
(4) 盗まれた (⇒p.59)　(5) を紹介した (⇒p.57)

3 (1) million (⇒p.62)　(2) boring (⇒p.84)　(3) tastes (⇒p.56)
(4) usual (⇒p.86)　(5) cross (⇒p.52)　(6) fly (⇒p.55)
(7) experience (⇒p.66)

4 (1) wide／広い (⇒p.86)　(2) expensive／高価な (⇒p.82)
(3) forget／を忘れる (⇒p.55)

でる度

A
B
C

単語編

差がつく応用単語 300

- 動詞 (67語) ······ 94
- 名詞 (161語) ······ 103
- 形容詞・副詞・その他 (72語) ··· 124
- チェックテスト ······ 134
- 過去問にチャレンジ！① ······ 136

でる度Cは、試験に出る頻度は下がりますが、いざというときに差がつく単語です。ここに掲載されている300語を覚えれば、3級レベルの語彙はばっちりです。

	1周目	2周目	3周目
動	/	/	/
名	/	/	/
形・副・他	/	/	/

でる度 C 差がつく応用単語

動詞　67語

🎧 0601〜0615

0601
attend
アテンド
[əténd]

[に出席する]
▶ attend the class　授業に出席する

0602
cancel
キャンセる
[kǽns(ə)l]

[を取り消す]
▶ All flights have been canceled.
全便が欠航になった。

0603
climb
クらイム
[klaim]　入試

[(に)登る]
▶ climb Mount Everest　エベレスト山に登る

0604
cut
カット
[kʌt]　入試

[を切る]
▶ cut a cake with a knife
ナイフでケーキを切る
★ [過去・過分] cut

0605
design
ディザイン
[dizáin]

[をデザインする]
▶ a shirt designed by a famous designer
有名なデザイナーによってデザインされたシャツ
🔖 デザイン

0606
hang
ハング
[hæŋ]

[を掛ける]
▶ hang a picture on the wall
壁に絵を掛ける
★ [過去・過分] hung

0607
knock
ナ(ー)ック
[nɑ(:)k]

[ノックする]
▶ knock on the door　ドアをノックする

0608 let
レット [let] 入試

[に〜させる]
- Let me introduce myself.
  自己紹介をさせてください。
- ★ let + (人) + (動詞の原形) で用いる

0609 oversleep
オウヴァスリープ [òuvərslíːp]

[寝過ごす]
- I overslept this morning. 今朝寝過ごした。
- ★ [過去・過分] overslept

0610 prepare
プリペア [pripéər] 入試

[準備する〈for 〜 〜を〉]
- prepare for the exam 試験の準備をする

0611 raise
レイズ [reiz]

[を上げる，を育てる]
- raise my hand 手を挙げる

0612 repeat
リピート [ripíːt]

[(を)繰り返す]
- Could you repeat that, please?
  もう一度言っていただけますか。

0613 rise
ライズ [raiz] 入試

[(太陽，月などが)昇る，上がる]
- The sun rose. 太陽が昇った。
- ⇔ set 沈む　★ 他動詞 raise との違いに注意
- ★ [過去] rose　[過分] risen

0614 seem
スィーム [siːm] 入試

[のように思われる]
- He seems to know the truth.
  彼は真実を知っているようだ。

0615 smile
スマイる [smail]

[ほほえむ〈at〜 〜に〉]
- She smiled at me.
  彼女が私にほほえみかけた。

---

have been canceled という言い方がリスニングで出やすいよ。

0616 touch
タッチ [tʌtʃ] 入試

[に触る]
► Don't touch it. それに触らないで。

0617 wonder
ワンダァ [wʌ́ndər]

[〜だろうかと思う]
► wonder what to wear 何を着ようかと思う
★ wonder +（疑問詞）でよく使われる

0618 act
アクト [ækt]

[(を)演じる，行動する]
► act in a play 劇で演じる
派 actor 名 俳優，男優　actress 名 女優

0619 add
アッド [æd]

[を加える]
► add sugar to coffee コーヒーに砂糖を加える
派 addition 名 追加
★ add A to B の形でよく使われる

0620 appear
アピア [əpíər]

[現れる]
► He finally appeared at the party.
ついに彼がパーティーに現れた。
⇔ disappear 存在しなくなる

0621 arrest
アレスト [ərést]

[を逮捕する]
► The man was arrested.
その男は逮捕された。

0622 boil
ボイる [bɔil]

[をゆでる]
► a boiled egg ゆで卵

0623 burn
バ〜ン [bəːrn]

[燃える，を燃やす]
► The house was burning. 家が燃えていた。
名 やけど
★ [過去・過分] burned, burnt

0624
cause
コーズ
[kɔːz]
🔒入試

[を引き起こす，の原因となる]
► cause global warming
　地球温暖化を引き起こす
★ by とともに受身形でもよく使われる

0625
cheer
チア
[tʃiər]

[を元気づける]
► cheer up Ron　ロンを元気づける
派 cheerful 形 元気のよい，陽気な
★ cheer ～ up で「～を元気づける」

0626
communicate
コミューニケイト
[kəmjúːnikeit]
🔒入試

[意思を通じ合わす，を伝える]
► communicate with each other
　互いに意思を伝え合う
派 communication 名 コミュニケーション

0627
control
コントゥロウる
[kəntróul]

[を制御する]
► control a robot　ロボットを操る
名 制御，コントロール

0628
decorate
デコレイト
[dékəreit]

[を飾る，を装飾する]
► decorate a Christmas tree
　クリスマスツリーを飾り付ける
派 decoration 名 飾り，装飾

0629
direct
ディレクト
[dərékt]

[を監督する]
► a movie directed by Mr. Smith
　スミス氏が監督した映画
派 director 名 (映画などの)監督

0630
disappear
ディサピア
[dìsəpíər]

[存在しなくなる]
► These birds are disappearing.
　この鳥は絶滅しつつある。
⇔ appear 現れる

0631
discover
ディスカヴァ
[diskʌ́vər]

[を発見する]
► discover an island　島を発見する

0632
escape
イスケイプ
[iskéip]

[逃げる]
▶ escape from enemies 敵から逃げる

0633
explain
イクスプれイン
[ikspléin] 入試

[(を)説明する]
▶ Could you explain that again?
もう一度それを説明していただけますか。
派 explanation 名 説明

0634
express
イクスプレス
[iksprés]

[を表現する]
▶ express feelings 感情を表現する
形 急行の 名 急行
派 expression 名 表現

0635
fail
ふエイル
[feil]

[(試験)に落ちる，失敗する]
▶ I failed the exam. 試験に落ちた。
⇔ pass に合格する

0636
feed
ふィード
[fi:d]

[に食べ物を与える]
▶ feed my cat 猫にえさをあげる
派 food 名 食べ物，料理
★ [過去・過分] fed

0637
fix
ふィックス
[fiks]

[を修理する]
▶ fix the broken car 壊れた車を修理する
≒ repair を修理する

0638
fold
ふオウるド
[fould]

[を折り畳む]
▶ fold it into four それを4つに折り畳む

0639
greet
グリート
[gri:t]

[にあいさつする]
▶ greet her with a smile
彼女に笑顔であいさつする
派 greeting 名 あいさつ

0640 hide
ハイド [haid] 入試

[隠れる，を隠す]
► hide behind the tree 木の陰に隠れる
★ [過去] hid [過分] hidden, hid

0641 hike
ハイク [haik]

[ハイキングをする]
► go hiking ハイキングに行く
名 ハイキング

0642 hunt
ハント [hʌnt]

[(の)狩りをする]
► hunt bears クマを狩る
派 hunting 名 狩り　hunter 名 猟師

0643 impress
インプレス [imprés]

[に印象づける，に感銘を与える]
► I was impressed with his speech.
　彼のスピーチには感心しました。
派 impressive 形 印象的な

0644 injure
インヂャ [índʒər]

[にけがをさせる]
► Many people were injured.
　多くの人が負傷した。
★ injured people で「負傷した人々」

0645 interview
インタヴュー [íntərvju:]

[にインタビューする]
► I interviewed the singer.
　その歌手にインタビューした。
名 インタビュー，面接

0646 judge
ヂャッヂ [dʒʌdʒ]

[(を)判断する]
► judge by the results 結果で判断する

0647 laugh
らふ [læf] 入試

[笑う]
► laugh a lot 大いに笑う

fold と hold を混同しないようにね。

0648
lay
れイ
[lei]

[(卵)を産む, を横たえる]
► Corals lay eggs. サンゴは卵を産む。
★ lay は lie(横たわる)の過去形と同じ形
★ [過去・過分] laid

0649
lead
リード
[li:d]

[を導く]
► lead the team チームを導く
派 leader 名 指導者, リーダー
★ [過去・過分] led

0650
marry
メリィ
[méri]
入試

[(と)結婚する]
► marry him 彼と結婚する
★ get married (to ~) で「(~と)結婚する」の意味

0651
mix
ミックス
[miks]

[を混ぜる, 混ざる]
► mix butter and sugar
バターと砂糖を混ぜる

0652
offer
オ(ー)ふァ
[ɔ́(:)fər]

[を提供する]
► offer some buses バスを数台提供する

0653
produce
プロドゥース
[prədú:s]

[を生産する]
► They produce cars.
彼らは車を生産している。
派 product 名 生産物

0654
pull
プる
[pul]
入試

[(を)引く]
► pull a rope ロープを引く
⇔ push (を)押す

0655
realize
リ(ー)アらイズ
[rí(:)əlaiz]
入試

[と気づく]
► realize that math is interesting
数学がおもしろいと気づく

0656
record
リコード
[rikɔ́ːrd]

[を録画[録音]する，を記録する]
▶ record my voice on tape
　自分の声をテープに録音する
图 記録 [rékərd レカァド]

0657
recycle
リーサイクる
[rìːsáikl]

[を再利用する]
▶ recycle bottles　びんを再利用する
派 recycling 图 再利用
★「を再使用する」は reuse

0658
shine
シャイン
[ʃain]

[輝く]
▶ The sun is shining.　太陽が輝いている。

0659
shock
シャ(ー)ック
[ʃɑ(ː)k]

[にショックを与える]
▶ I was shocked to hear that.
　私はそれを聞いてショックを受けた。
图 (精神的な)打撃，ショック

0660
shoot
シュート
[ʃuːt]

[(弾丸・矢で)(を)撃つ]
▶ shoot a bird　鳥を射る
★[過去・過分] shot

0661
smoke
スモウク
[smouk]

[タバコを吸う]
▶ stop smoking　たばこをやめる
图 煙

0662
solve
サ(ー)るヴ
[sɑ(ː)lv]

[を解く]
▶ solve a problem　問題を解く

入試

0663
spell
スぺる
[spel]

[をつづる]
▶ How do you spell that word?
　その語はどうつづりますか。
派 spelling 图 つづり，スペル

0664

support
サポート
[səpɔ́ːrt]

[を支える，を支援する]
▶ support the project
　プロジェクトを支援する
图 支持，支援

0665

survive
サヴァイヴ
[sərváiv]

[(を)生き残る]
▶ survive the war　戦争を生き残る
派 survival 图 生き残ること

0666

waste
ウェイスト
[weist]

[を無駄に使う]
▶ Don't waste the money.
　お金の無駄遣いをしてはいけません。
图 無駄，廃棄物

0667

wish
ウィッシ
[wiʃ]

[(を)望む 〈for〉]
▶ wish for world peace　世界平和を望む
图 願い，望み
★make a wish で「願い事をする」

でる度 C 差がつく応用単語

名詞　161語

🎧 0668～0674

0668
activity
アクティヴィティ
[æktívəti]　入試

[活動]
▶ club activities クラブ活動
派 active 形 活動的な

0669
address
アドゥレス
[ədrés]

[住所，（メールの）アドレス]
▶ Write your name and address here.
ここに名前と住所を書いてください。

0670
adult
アダルト
[ədʌ́lt]

[大人]
▶ from children to adults
子どもから大人まで
⇔ child 子ども

0671
age
エイヂ
[eidʒ]　入試

[年齢]
▶ at the age of 20　20歳で

0672
apartment
アパートメント
[əpáːrtmənt]

[アパート]
▶ live in a small apartment
小さなアパートに住む

0673
aquarium
アクウェ（ア）リアム
[əkwé(ə)riəm]

[水族館]
▶ dolphins in the aquarium 水族館のイルカ

0674
arm
アーム
[ɑːrm]　入試

[腕]
▶ hurt my arm 腕をけがする

日本語の「マンション」も apartment と言うよ。

0675
basket
バスケット
[bǽskət]

[かご]
▶ oranges in a basket かごの中のオレンジ

0676
battle
バトゥる
[bǽtl]

[戦い]
▶ win a battle 戦いに勝つ

0677
block
ブら(ー)ック
[blɑ(:)k]

[(街の)1区画]
▶ walk two blocks along the street
通りに沿って2区画歩く

0678
body
バ(ー)ディ
[bá(:)di]   入試

[体]
▶ a healthy body 健康的な体

0679
business
ビズネス
[bíznəs]   入試

[仕事, 商売]
▶ Mike is on a business trip.
マイクは出張中です。

0680
button
バトゥン
[bʌ́t(ə)n]

[押しボタン, (服の)ボタン]
▶ press a button ボタンを押す

0681
ceiling
スィーりンヶ
[sí:liŋ]

[天井]
▶ a hole in the ceiling 天井に開いた穴

0682
centimeter
センティミータァ
[séntəmì:tər]

[センチメートル]
▶ It's fifty centimeters long.
それは長さ50センチです。
★「ミリメートル」は millimeter

0683
ceremony
セレモウニィ
[sérəmouni]

[儀式]
► a wedding ceremony 結婚式

0684
chef
シェふ
[ʃef]

[シェフ, コック長]
► work as a restaurant chef
レストランのシェフとして働く
★ cook は単に「料理をする人」で, chef は職業

0685
closet
クら(ー)ゼット
[klá(:)zət]

[押し入れ, 戸棚]
► clothes in the closet 押し入れの服

0686
corner
コーナァ
[kɔ́ːrnər]

[角]
► Turn right at the next corner.
次の角を右に曲がってください。

0687
costume
カ(ー)ストゥーム
[ká(:)stuːm]

[衣装]
► a Halloween costume ハロウィーンの衣装

0688
custom
カスタム
[kʌ́stəm]

[慣習]
► Japanese customs 日本の慣習

0689
department store
ディパートメント ストー
[dipáːrtmənt stɔːr]

[デパート]
► go to the department store
デパートへ行く

0690
difference
ディふ(ァ)レンス
[díf(ə)r(ə)ns]

[違い]
► differences between Japan and Korea
日本と韓国の違い
派 different 形 異なった, 別の, さまざまな

0691 director
ディレクタァ [dəréktər]
[(映画などの)監督]
▶ a movie director 映画監督
派 direct 動 を監督する

0692 drugstore
ドゥラグストー [drʌ́gstɔːr]
[ドラッグストア, 薬局]
▶ buy some medicine at the drugstore ドラッグストアで薬を買う

0693 fever
ふィーヴァ [fíːvər]
[(病気の)熱]
▶ have a fever 熱がある

0694 field
ふィールド [fíːld]
入試
[野原, 田畑]
▶ play in the field 野原で遊ぶ

0695 figure
ふィギャ [fígjər]
[図]
▶ See Figure 1. 図1参照。

0696 flight
ふらイト [fláit]
[飛行機の便, 飛行]
▶ flights to Europe ヨーロッパ行きの便
派 fly 動 飛行機で行く, 飛ぶ

0697 furniture
ふァ〜ニチャ [fə́ːrnitʃər]
[家具]
▶ go to the furniture shop 家具店へ行く

0698 garbage
ガービヂ [gáːrbidʒ]
入試
[ごみ]
▶ a garbage bag ごみ袋

0699
grandson
グラン(ド)サン
[grǽn(d)sʌ̀n]

[孫息子]
► He has a grandson. 彼には孫息子がいる。
⇔ granddaughter 孫娘

0700
grass
グラス
[grǽs]

[草, 芝生]
► sit on the grass 草の上に座る
★ glass (コップ) と混同しないように

0701
guide
ガイド
[gáid]
入試

[案内人, ガイド]
► a tour guide ツアーガイド

0702
hallway
ホールウェイ
[hɔ́ːlwei]

[廊下]
► run in the hallway 廊下を走る

0703
hero
ヒーロウ
[híːrou]

[英雄, (男性の)主人公]
► heroes in the world 世界の英雄たち
⇔ heroine 女主人公, ヒロイン

0704
holiday
ハ(ー)リデイ
[hɑ́(ː)lədei]

[休日, 祝日]
► a national holiday 国民の休日

0705
horizon
ホライズン
[həráiz(ə)n]

[地平線, 水平線]
► above the horizon 水平線上に

0706
illness
イるネス
[ílnəs]

[病気]
► a serious illness 深刻な病気
≒ sickness 病気
派 ill 形 病気の

0707
list
リスト
[list]

[一覧表, リスト]
▶ find his name in the list
リストに彼の名前を見つける

0708
memory
メモリィ
[mém(ə)ri]　🔒入試

[思い出]
▶ have good memories of school life
学校生活のよい思い出がある

0709
middle
ミドゥる
[mídl]

[真ん中]
▶ the boy standing in the middle
真ん中に立っている男の子

0710
midnight
ミッドナイト
[mídnait]

[(深夜の)12時, 真夜中]
▶ I woke up at midnight.
私は真夜中に目が覚めた。

0711
model
マ(ー)ドゥる
[má(:)dl]

[型, 模型]
▶ an old model 古い型

0712
musical
ミューズィカる
[mjú:zik(ə)l]

[ミュージカル]
▶ perform a musical at a hall
ホールでミュージカルを上演する
形 音楽の

0713
neighborhood
ネイバフッド
[néibərhud]

[近所]
▶ in my neighborhood
私の家の近所で

0714
noon
ヌーン
[nu:n]

[正午]
▶ Let's meet at noon. 正午に会いましょう。

0715
opinion
オピニョン
[əpínjən]

[意見]
▶ in my opinion 私の意見では

0716
oven
アヴン
[ʌ́v(ə)n]

[オーブン]
▶ Put the pizza in the oven.
ピザをオーブンに入れてちょうだい。
★「オーヴン」とは発音しない

0717
pajamas
パヂャーマズ
[pədʒáːməz]

[(複数扱いで)パジャマ]
▶ a pair of pajamas パジャマ1着

0718
planet
プラネット
[plǽnit]

[惑星]
▶ the nearest planet to the sun
太陽に最も近い惑星
★ star は「恒星」

0719
pleasure
プレジャ
[pléʒər]

[喜び]
▶ My pleasure. どういたしまして。
派 pleased 形 うれしい

0720
pocket
パ(ー)ケット
[pá(ː)kət]

[ポケット]
▶ look in the pocket of the jacket
上着のポケットの中を見る

0721
police
ポリース
[pəlíːs]

[警察]
▶ a police officer 警察官

0722
puppy
パピィ
[pʌ́pi]

[子犬]
▶ have a puppy 子犬を飼う
★「子猫」は kitten, small dog は「小型犬」

musical instrument は「音楽の器具＝楽器」だね。

0723	**radio** レイディオウ [réidiou]	[ラジオ] ▶ hear the news on the radio ラジオでニュースを聞く
0724	**schedule** スケヂューる [skédʒuːl]	[予定] ▶ check my schedule 自分のスケジュールをチェックする
0725	**score** スコー [skɔːr]	[点数] ▶ get a perfect score 満点を取る 動 (点)を取る
0726	**shuttle** シャトゥる [ʃʌtl]	[往復便] ▶ a shuttle bus シャトル[近距離往復]バス ★「スペースシャトル」は space shuttle
0727	**sight** サイト [sait]	[視力, 視覚] ▶ He is losing his sight. 彼は視力が弱っています。
0728	**sofa** ソウふァ [sóufə]	[ソファ] ▶ the woman sitting on a sofa ソファに座っている女性
0729	**storm** ストーム [stɔːrm]	[嵐, 暴風雨] ▶ because of the storm 暴風雨のために
0730	**tie** タイ [tai]	[ネクタイ, ひも] ▶ the man wearing a tie ネクタイをしている男性

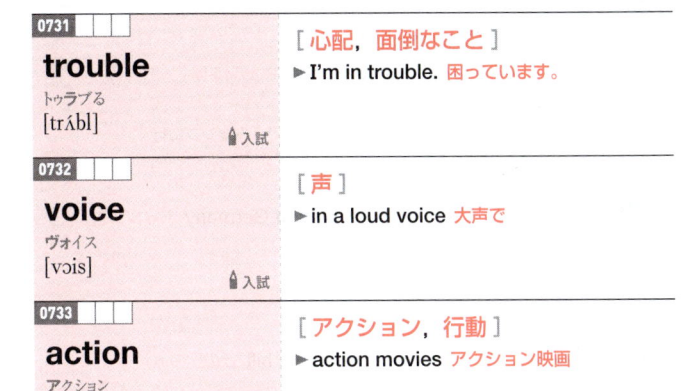

0731 trouble
トゥラブる [trʌ́bl] 入試

[心配, 面倒なこと]
► I'm in trouble. 困っています。

0732 voice
ヴォイス [vɔis] 入試

[声]
► in a loud voice 大声で

0733 action
アクション [ǽkʃ(ə)n]

[アクション, 行動]
► action movies アクション映画

0734 advice
アドヴァイス [ədváis] 入試

[助言]
► Give me a piece of advice. ひと言, 助言をください。
派 advise 動 に助言する

0735 award
アウォード [əwɔ́ːrd]

[賞]
► win an award 賞を勝ち取る
動 (賞)を与える
≒ prize 賞

0736 beginning
ビギニング [bigíniŋ]

[初め]
► at the beginning of July 7月の初めに
⇔ end 終わり

0737 billion
ビリョン [bíljən]

[10億]
► about two billion people 約20億人

0738 blackboard
ブラックボード [blǽkbɔːrd]

[黒板]
► Look at the blackboard. 黒板を見なさい。
★ 単に board とも言う

0739
camp
キャンプ
[kæmp]
入試

[キャンプ]
► a camp site キャンプ場
動 キャンプする
★go camping で「キャンプに行く」

0740
capital
キャピトゥる
[kǽpət(ə)l]

[首都]
► the capital of Germany ドイツの首都

0741
castle
キャスる
[kǽsl]

[城]
► a castle on a hill 丘の上の城

0742
climate
クらイメット
[kláimət]

[気候]
► a mild climate 穏やかな気候
★「天気, 天候」は weather

0743
comic
カ(ー)ミック
[ká(:)mik]

[漫画本]
► read comics 漫画本を読む
★comic book とも言う

0744
communication
コミューニケイション
[kəmjù:nikéiʃ(ə)n]

[コミュニケーション]
► a good tool for communication
コミュニケーションによい手段
派 communicate 動 意思を通じ合わす, を伝える

0745
damage
ダメッヂ
[dǽmidʒ]

[損害, 被害]
► damage by Hurricane Katrina
ハリケーン・カトリーナによる被害
動 に損害を与える

0746
danger
デインヂャ
[déindʒər]

[危険]
► in danger 危険な状態で
派 dangerous 形 危険な

0747
death
デス
[deθ]

[死, 死亡]
▶ after his death 彼の死後
派 die 動 死ぬ　dead 形 死んでいる

0748
desert
デザト
[dézərt]

[砂漠]
▶ the Sahara Desert サハラ砂漠
★dessert（デザート）と混同しないように

0749
difficulty
ディふィクるティ
[dífik(ə)lti]

[困難]
▶ have difficulty in solving the problem
　問題を解決するのに苦労する
派 difficult 形 難しい

0750
earthquake
ア～すクウェイク
[ə́:rθkweik]

[地震]
▶ We had an earthquake. 地震があった。

0751
elevator
エれヴェイタァ
[éliveitər]

[エレベーター]
▶ go up in an elevator
　エレベーターで上階へ行く
★「エスカレーター」は escalator

0752
enemy
エネミィ
[énəmi]

[敵]
▶ attack enemies 敵を攻撃する

0753
energy
エナヂィ
[énərdʒi]
入試

[エネルギー]
▶ need a lot of energy
　多くのエネルギーを必要とする

0754
examination
イグザミネイション
[igzæminéiʃ(ə)n]

[試験]
▶ an entrance examination 入学試験
= exam

desert と dessert（72ページ）のつづりと発音に注意。

0755 expression
イクスプレション [ikspréʃ(ə)n]

[表現]
▶ a useful expression 役立つ表現
派 express 動 を表現する 形 急行の 名 急行

0756 firework
ふァイアワ～ク [fáiərwəːrk]

[(通常複数形で)花火]
▶ go and see fireworks 花火を見に行く

0757 flag
ふらッグ [flæg]

[旗]
▶ a national flag 国旗

0758 fork
ふォーク [fɔːrk]

[フォーク]
▶ a knife and fork ナイフとフォーク

0759 freedom
ふリーダム [fríːdəm]

[自由]
▶ fight for freedom 自由のために戦う
派 free 形 自由な

0760 fridge
ふリッヂ [fridʒ]

[冷蔵庫]
▶ Look in the fridge.
冷蔵庫の中を見てごらん。
★refrigerator の略で，会話では fridge と言う

0761 friendship
ふレンドシップ [fréndʃip]

[友情，友好関係]
▶ friendship between two countries
二国間の友好関係

0762 generation
ヂェネレイション [dʒènəréiʃ(ə)n]

[世代，同世代の人々]
▶ the next generation 次世代

0763 gesture
チェスチャ [dʒéstʃər]

[身ぶり]
► express myself with gesture 身ぶりで表現する

0764 glass
グラス [glæs] 🔒入試

[コップ，ガラス]
► a glass of water コップ1杯の水
★ 複数形 glasses は「めがね」

0765 glove
グラヴ [glʌv]

[(通常複数形で)手袋]
► a pair of gloves 1組の手袋

0766 gram
グラム [græm]

[グラム]
► 100 grams of sugar 100グラムの砂糖
★「キログラム」は kilogram

0767 grandparent
グラン(ド)ペ(ア)レント [grǽn(d)pè(ə)r(ə)nt]

[祖父，祖母]
► visit my grandparents 祖父母を訪ねる

0768 greeting
グリーティング [gríːtiŋ]

[あいさつ]
► a greeting card （クリスマスや誕生日の）あいさつ状
派 greet 動 にあいさつする

0769 heat
ヒート [hiːt]

[熱，暑さ]
► the sun's heat 太陽の熱
動 を熱する，を温める，温まる

0770 hint
ヒント [hint]

[ヒント]
► Give me a hint. ヒントをください。

0771
hole
ホウる
[houl]
入試

[穴]
▶ look into the hole 穴の中をのぞきこむ

0772
horse
ホース
[hɔːrs]
入試

[馬]
▶ ride a horse 馬に乗る

0773
host
ホウスト
[houst]
入試

[(客をもてなす)主人]
▶ my host family 私のホストファミリー

0774
importance
インポータンス
[impɔ́ːrt(ə)ns]

[重要性]
▶ the importance of communication コミュニケーションの重要性
派 important 形 重要な

0775
ink
インク
[iŋk]

[インク]
▶ in red ink 赤インクで

0776
juice
ヂュース
[dʒuːs]

[(果物・野菜の)ジュース]
▶ a glass of orange juice コップ１杯のオレンジジュース

0777
leaf
りーふ
[liːf]

[葉]
▶ autumn leaves 紅葉
★ [複数形] leaves

0778
license
らイセンス
[láis(ə)ns]

[免許]
▶ a driver's license 運転免許証

0779 mirror
ミラァ [mírər]

[鏡]
► look at myself in the mirror
鏡に映った自分を見る

0780 neighbor
ネイバァ [néibər]

[近所の人]
► My neighbors are friendly.
近所の人たちは親しみやすい。

0781 nephew
ネふューー [néfju:]

[おい]
► My nephew is an anime fan.
私のおいはアニメファンだ。
⇔ niece めい

0782 noise
ノイズ [nɔiz]

[騒音]
► the noise of a plane 飛行機の騒音
派 noisy 形 騒がしい

0783 note
ノウト [nout]

[メモ，短い手紙]
► take notes メモをとる

0784 novel
ナ(ー)ヴ(ェ)る [ná(:)v(ə)l]

[(長編)小説]
► a character in a novel 小説の中の登場人物
派 novelist 名 小説家

0785 oil
オイる [ɔil]

[油]
► Oil doesn't mix with water.
油は水と混ざらない。

0786 owner
オウナァ [óunər]

[所有者]
► a pet owner ペットの飼い主
派 own 形 自分自身の 動 を所有する

neighborhood はふつう地域，neighbor は人を指すよ。

0787
pain
ペイン
[pein]

[痛み]
▶ have a pain in the back 背中が痛む

0788
passenger
パセンヂャ
[pǽsindʒər]

[乗客]
▶ All the passengers got off the train.
全乗客が列車を降りた。

0789
peace
ピース
[piːs]

[平和]
▶ world peace 世界平和
⇔ war 戦争
派 peaceful 形 平和な

0790
performance
パふォーマンス
[pərfɔ́ːrməns]

[公演, 演技]
▶ have two performances a day
1日2回公演がある
派 perform 動 を上演する, (を)演じる

0791
port
ポート
[pɔːrt]

[港]
▶ the port of Seattle シアトル港

0792
postcard
ポウス(ト)カード
[póus(t)kɑːrd]

[はがき]
▶ a picture postcard 絵はがき

0793
program
プロウグラム
[próugræm] 入試

[番組, 計画]
▶ an interesting TV program
おもしろいテレビ番組

0794
resort
リゾート
[rizɔ́ːrt]

[行楽地]
▶ a ski resort スキーリゾート(地)

0795
rocket
ラ(ー)ケット
[rá(ː)kət]

[ロケット]
► make rockets ロケットを作る

0796
sadness
サッドネス
[sǽdnəs]

[悲しみ]
► feel sadness 悲しみを感じる
派 sad 形 悲しい

0797
safety
セイふティ
[séifti]

[安全]
► a safety belt 安全ベルト
派 safe 形 安全な　safely 副 安全に

0798
salesclerk
セイるズクら〜ク
[séilzklə:rk]

[店員，販売員]
► ask the salesclerk 店員にたずねる
★ clerk とも言う

0799
scene
スィーン
[siːn]

[場面]
► the last scene 最後の場面

0800
scissors
スィザズ
[sízərz]

[(複数扱いで) はさみ]
► a pair of scissors はさみ1丁

0801
shampoo
シャンプー
[ʃæmpúː]

[シャンプー]
► shampoo and conditioner
　シャンプーとコンディショナー
★「リンス」と言わず conditioner と言う

0802
shape
シェイプ
[ʃeip]

[形]
► round in shape 形が丸い

---

sadness や illness など -ness は形容詞を名詞にするよ。

0803		
shower シャウア [ʃáuər]	[シャワー，にわか雨] ▶ take a shower シャワーを浴びる	

0804		
shrine シライン [ʃrain]	[神社] ▶ visit a shrine on New Year's Day 元日に神社を訪れる ★「寺」は temple	

0805		
sightseeing サイトスィーイング [sáitsi:iŋ]	[観光] ▶ visit Korea for sightseeing 観光で韓国に行く	

0806		
skill スキる [skil]	[技術] ▶ learn skills 技術を学ぶ	

0807		
sneaker スニーカァ [sní:kər]	[(通常複数形で)スニーカー] ▶ a pair of sneakers スニーカー1足	

0808		
soldier ソウるヂャ [sóuldʒər]	[(陸軍の)兵士，軍人] ▶ soldiers killed in a war 戦死した兵士たち	

0809		
speed スピード [spi:d]	[速度] ▶ run at full speed 全速力で走る	

0810		
stadium ステイディアム [stéidiəm]	[スタジアム，競技場] ▶ a soccer stadium サッカー競技場	

0811
stair
ステア
[steər]

[（通常複数形で）階段]
► go up the stairs 階段を上がる

0812
state
ステイト
[steit]

[（アメリカなどの）州]
► New York State ニューヨーク州

0813
statue
スタチュー
[stǽtʃuː]

[像, 彫像]
► the Statue of Liberty 自由の女神像

0814
steak
ステイク
[steik]

[ステーキ]
► How would you like your steak?
ステーキの焼き加減はいかがいたしますか。

0815
stomach
スタマック
[stʌ́mək]

[胃, 腹]
► My stomach hurts. 胃が痛い。

0816
stranger
ストゥレインヂャ
[stréindʒər]

[見知らぬ人, （その土地に）初めて来た人]
► I'm a stranger here.
私はここのことはよくわかりません。

0817
sugar
シュガァ
[ʃúgər]

[砂糖]
► sugar and salt 砂糖と塩

0818
suit
スート
[suːt]

[スーツ]
► the man in a suit スーツを着た男性
動 （色などが）に似合う

0819
suitcase
スートケイス
[súːtkeis]

[スーツケース]
► carry the suitcase スーツケースを運ぶ

0820
sunrise
サンライズ
[sʌ́nraiz]

[日の出]
► leave before sunrise 日の出前に出発する
⇔ sunset 日没

0821
sunset
サンセット
[sʌ́nset]

[日没]
► the sunset sky 夕方の空
⇔ sunrise 日の出

0822
symbol
スィンボる
[símb(ə)l]

[象徴]
► a symbol of peace 平和の象徴

0823
temperature
テンペラチャ
[témp(ə)rətʃər]

[温度, 体温]
► take my temperature 体温を測る

0824
tradition
トゥラディション
[trədíʃ(ə)n]

[伝統]
► The tradition began in the 10th century.
  その伝統は 10 世紀に始まった。
派 traditional 形 伝統的な

0825
twin
トゥウィン
[twin]

[(複数形で)ふたご]
► They are twins. 彼らはふたごだ。

0826
typhoon
タイふーン
[taifúːn]

[台風]
► stay home during the typhoon
  台風の間, 家にいる
★「ハリケーン」は hurricane

0827	**wine** ワイン [wain]	[ワイン] ▶ a glass of wine　グラス1杯のワイン
0828	**wing** ウィング [wiŋ]	[（鳥・飛行機などの）つばさ] ▶ the wings of a plane　飛行機のつばさ

sunrise は sun（太陽）+ rise（昇る）ということだね。

でる度 C 差がつく応用単語

形容詞・副詞・その他 72語

🎧 0829〜0843

0829 asleep
アスリープ
[əslíːp]

形 [眠って]
▶ fall asleep 眠りにつく

0830 bright
ブライト
[brait]

形 [明るい]
▶ make the room brighter
部屋をもっと明るくする

0831 careful
ケアふる
[kéərfəl] 入試

形 [注意深い]
▶ Be careful. 気をつけて。
派 carefully 副 注意深く
　care 名 世話, 注意 動 気にする, 心配する

0832 central
セントゥラる
[séntr(ə)l]

形 [中央の]
▶ Central America 中央アメリカ
派 center 名 中心(地), センター

0833 clever
クれヴァ
[klévər]

形 [利口な]
▶ a clever dog 利口な犬

0834 comfortable
カンふォタブる
[kʌ́mfərtəbl]

形 [心地よい]
▶ a comfortable sofa 座り心地のよいソファ

0835 common
カ(ー)モン
[ká(ː)mən]

形 [一般的な, 共通の]
▶ a common mistake よくある間違い

0836 cute
キュート [kjuːt]
形 [かわいい]
▶ a cute girl かわいい女の子

0837 dark
ダーク [dɑːrk] 入試
形 [暗い]
▶ It's getting dark. 暗くなりつつある。

0838 digital
ディヂトゥる [dídʒit(ə)l]
形 [デジタル（方式）の]
▶ a digital camera デジタルカメラ

0839 excellent
エクセれント [éks(ə)lənt]
形 [優れた，立派な]
▶ an excellent performance 優れた演技

0840 friendly
ふレンドりィ [fréndli] 入試
形 [親しみやすい，親切な]
▶ friendly people 親しみやすい人々
★ 語尾が -ly でも形容詞

0841 healthy
へるすィ [hélθi] 入試
形 [健康的な]
▶ healthy food 健康的な食べ物
派 health 名 健康

0842 latest
れイテスト [léitist]
形 [最新の]
▶ the latest video game 最新のテレビゲーム
★ late「遅い」の最上級の１つ

0843 local
ろウカる [lóuk(ə)l]
形 [地元の]
▶ local food 地元の食べ物

0844 natural
ナチ(ュ)らる
[nǽtʃ(ə)r(ə)l] 入試

形 [自然の]
► natural gas 天然ガス
派 nature 名 自然

0845 necessary
ネセセリィ
[nésəseri]

形 [必要な]
► necessary for health 健康に不可欠な
派 need 動 を必要とする

0846 quiet
クワイエット
[kwáiət] 入試

形 [静かな]
► Be quiet. 静かにしなさい。
⇔ loud (声・音が)大きい

0847 round
ラウンド
[raund]

形 [丸い]
► The earth is round. 地球は丸い。

0848 scared
スケアド
[skeərd]

形 [おびえた]
► She looked scared.
　彼女はおびえているように見えた。
≒ afraid 怖がって

0849 several
セヴらる
[sévr(ə)l] 入試

形 [いくつかの]
► several times 数回

0850 simple
スィンプる
[símpl]

形 [簡単な, 単純な]
► in simple English 簡単な英語で

0851 snowy
スノウイ
[snóui]

形 [雪の多い, 雪の積もった]
► in the snowy season 雪の多い季節に
派 snow 動 雪が降る 名 雪

0852 southern
サザン [sʌ́ðərn]

形 [南(部)の]
▶ the Southern States アメリカ南部諸州
⇔ northern 北(部)の
派 south 名 南

0853 strong
ストゥロ(ー)ング [strɔ(:)ŋ] 入試

形 [強い]
▶ a strong team 強いチーム
⇔ weak 弱い

0854 sweet
スウィート [swi:t] 入試

形 [甘い]
▶ This flower smells sweet. この花は甘いにおいがする。
名 (sweets で)甘いお菓子

0855 thick
すィック [θik]

形 [厚い]
▶ a thick book 厚い本
⇔ thin 薄い

0856 thirsty
さ〜スティ [θə́:rsti]

形 [のどが乾いている]
▶ I'm thirsty. のどが乾いている。

0857 traditional
トゥラディショヌる [trədíʃ(ə)n(ə)l]

形 [伝統的な]
▶ a traditional event 伝統行事
派 tradition 名 伝統

0858 upset
アップセット [ʌpsét]

形 [気が動転した, うろたえた]
▶ She was upset about something. 彼女は何かにうろたえていた。

0859 whole
ホウる [houl]

形 [全体の]
▶ a whole day 丸一日

snow＜snowy 形, storm＜stormy 形 で覚えよう。

0860
alive
アらイヴ
[əláiv]

形 [生きている]
▶ The fish is alive. その魚は生きている。
⇔ dead 死んでいる

0861
cheerful
チアふる
[tʃíərf(ə)l]

形 [元気のよい，陽気な]
▶ She is always cheerful.
彼女はいつも元気だ。
派 cheer 動 を元気づける

0862
dirty
ダ～ティ
[də́ːrti]

形 [汚い，汚れた]
▶ dirty clothes 汚れた服
⇔ clean きれいな，清潔な

0863
elderly
エるダァリィ
[éldərli]

形 [年配の]
▶ elderly people 年配の人
★ old(年老いた)よりも丁寧な語
★ 語尾が -ly でも形容詞

0864
helpful
へるプふる
[hélpf(ə)l]

形 [役立つ]
▶ This book is helpful. この本は役立つ。
派 help 動 (を)助ける，役立つ 名 助け

0865
huge
ヒューヂ
[hjuːdʒ]

形 [非常に大きい]
▶ a huge rock 巨大な岩
= very big

0866
impossible
インパ(ー)スィブる
[impá(ː)səbl]

形 [不可能な]
▶ That's impossible. それは不可能だ。
⇔ possible 可能な

0867
international
インタナショヌる
[ìntərnǽʃ(ə)n(ə)l]

形 [国際的な]
▶ an international event 国際的なイベント

0868 lonely
ろウンりィ [lóunli]

形 [さびしい]
▶ live a lonely life さびしい生活を送る
★ 語尾が -ly でも形容詞

0869 low
ろウ [lou] 入試

形 [低い]
▶ This tree is lower than that one. この木はあの木よりも低い。
⇔ high 高い

0870 lucky
らキィ [lʌ́ki] 入試

形 [運のよい]
▶ You're lucky. 君は幸運だね。
派 luck 名 運, 幸運 luckily 副 幸運にも

0871 mild
マイるド [maild]

形 [温和な, 温暖な]
▶ mild weather 温暖な天候

0872 noisy
ノイズィ [nɔ́izi]

形 [騒がしい]
▶ noisy children 騒がしい子どもたち
派 noise 名 騒音

0873 official
オふィシャる [əfíʃ(ə)l]

形 [公式の]
▶ an official website 公式ウェブサイト

0874 outdoor
アウトドー [àutdɔ́ːr]

形 [屋外の]
▶ outdoor sports 屋外スポーツ
⇔ indoor 屋内の

0875 peaceful
ピースふる [píːsf(ə)l]

形 [平和な]
▶ a peaceful country 平和な国
派 peace 名 平和

0876 polite
ポライト
[pəláit]

形 [礼儀正しい]
▶ a polite student 礼儀正しい生徒
⇔ rude 無作法な

0877 powerful
パウアふる
[páuərf(ə)l]

形 [強力な]
▶ look powerful 強そうに見える
派 power 名 力

0878 serious
スィ(ア)リアス
[sí(ə)riəs]

形 [真剣な, 重大な]
▶ a serious problem 重大な問題

0879 surprising
サプライズィング
[sərpráiziŋ]

形 [驚くべき]
▶ a surprising result 驚くべき結果
★ surprised は「(人が)驚いた」

0880 tasty
テイスティ
[téisti]

形 [おいしい]
▶ It's tasty. おいしいです。
派 taste 動 の味がする 名 味

0881 tight
タイト
[tait]

形 [きつい]
▶ The shirt is a little tight. シャツが少しきつい。
派 tightly 副 しっかりと

0882 wet
ウェット
[wet]

形 [ぬれた]
▶ get wet ぬれる
⇔ dry 乾いた

0883 anytime
エニタイム
[énitaim]

副 [(肯定文で)いつでも]
▶ You can come anytime. いつでも来ていいよ。

0884
anyway
エニウェイ
[éniwei]

副 [とにかく]
► Thanks anyway. とにかくありがとう。

0885
anywhere
エニ(フ)ウェア
[éni(h)weər]

副 [(疑問文で)どこかへ [に]]
► Did you go anywhere? どこかへ行った？
★ 否定文で「どこへ [に] も (〜ない)」, 肯定文で「どこへ [に] でも」

0886
badly
バッドリィ
[bǽdli]

副 [ひどく]
► He's badly injured.
彼はひどくけがをしている。
派 bad 形 悪い, ひどい

0887
instead
インステッド
[instéd]

副 [代わりに]
► I had Chinese food instead.
代わりに中華料理を食べた。

0888
online
ア(ー)ンらイン
[à(:)nláin]

副 [オンラインで, インターネットで]
► get a ticket online
インターネットでチケットを入手する
形 オンラインの

0889
safely
セイふリィ
[séifli]

副 [安全に, 無事に]
► get home safely 無事に帰宅する
派 safe 形 安全な

0890
actually
アクチュ(ア)リィ
[ǽktʃu(ə)li]

副 [実のところ, 実際に]
► Actually, she is very nice.
実のところ, 彼女はとても親切だ。

0891
aloud
アらウド
[əláud]

副 [声を出して]
► read aloud 声を出して読む
★ loud は形容詞で「(声・音が) 大きい」

0892 carefully
ケアふりィ
[kéərfəli] 入試

副 [注意深く]
▶ look carefully 注意深く見る
派 careful 形 注意深い

0893 overseas
オウヴァスィーズ
[òuvərsíːz]

副 [海外へ[で]]
▶ work overseas 海外で働く
≒ abroad 海外へ[で]

0894 softly
ソ(ー)ふトりィ
[sɔ́(ː)ftli]

副 [優しく, 静かに]
▶ speak softly そっと話す
派 soft 形 柔らかい

0895 unfortunately
アンふォーチュネットりィ
[ʌnfɔ́ːrtʃ(ə)nətli]

副 [不幸にも]
▶ Unfortunately, it rained all day.
不幸にも, 一日中雨だった。
⇔ fortunately 幸運にも

0896 upstairs
アップステアズ
[ʌ̀pstéərz]

副 [上の階へ[に]]
▶ go upstairs 上階へ行く
⇔ downstairs 下の階へ[に]

0897 although
オーるぞウ
[ɔːlðóu]

接 [～だけれども]
▶ Although it was raining, she went for a walk.
雨が降っていたが, 彼女は散歩に出かけた。

0898 among
アマング
[əmʌ́ŋ] 入試

前 [(3つ[人]以上のもの)の中に[で]]
▶ popular among girls
女の子の間で人気がある
★ between は「2つのもの[人]の間に[で]」

0899 toward
トード
[tɔːrd] 入試

前 [の方へ]
▶ sail toward the east 東へ向かって航行する

0900

above

アバヴ
[əbʌ́v]

前 [の上に[へ]]

► The sun rose above the horizon.
太陽が地平線の上方に昇った。

★ on (の上に) は接触していることを表す

単語編は終わり！　ひと休みしよう。

単語編 でる度 **C**

チェックテスト

1 下線の語句の意味を①〜③の中から選びましょう。

(1) **attend** the class
　① を教える　② に出席する　③ を取り消す

(2) **discover** an island
　① を発明する　② を破壊する　③ を発見する

(3) sit on the **grass**　① 地面　② 草　③ 田畑

(4) **boil** an egg　① を加える　② をゆでる　③ を割る

(5) colorful autumn **leaves**　① 葉　② 人生　③ 出発

2 下線の単語の意味を答えましょう。

(1) **cancel** the meeting　　会合（　　　　　　　　）

(2) What's the **difference**?　（　　　　　　）は何ですか。

(3) wish for **peace**　　　　（　　　　　　）を望む

(4) a **polite** boy　　　　　（　　　　　　）男の子

(5) wash the **dirty** shoes　（　　　　　　）靴を洗う

3 日本語に合うように（　）に英単語を入れましょう。

(1) 山に登る　　　　　（　　　　　） a mountain

(2) 理由を説明する　　（　　　　　） the reason

(3) 太陽が昇った。　The sun（　　　　　）．

(4) 車でそこへ行くのは不可能だ。
It is（　　　　　） to get there by car.

(5) 傘を折り畳む　　　（　　　　　） an umbrella

(6) 大いに笑う　　　　（　　　　　） a lot

(7) 日本の伝統　　　　a Japanese（　　　　　）

4 下線の単語の反意語（⇔）とその意味を答えましょう。

(1) **pass** the exam　⇔　（　　　　　） the exam
　　　　　　　　　　　　　試験（　　　）

(2) at a **high** price　⇔　at a（　　　　　）price
　　　　　　　　　　　　　（　　　）価格で

(3) in a **loud** voice　⇔　in a（　　　　　）voice
　　　　　　　　　　　　　（　　　）声で

正解

1 (1) ②(⇒p.94)　(2) ③(⇒p.97)　(3) ②(⇒p.107)　(4) ②(⇒p.96)
(5) ①(⇒p.116)

2 (1) を取り消す(⇒p.94)　(2) 違い(⇒p.105)　(3) 平和(⇒p.118)
(4) 礼儀正しい(⇒p.130)　(5) 汚れた(⇒p.128)

3 (1) climb(⇒p.94)　(2) explain(⇒p.98)　(3) rose(⇒p.95)
(4) impossible(⇒p.128)　(5) fold(⇒p.98)　(6) laugh(⇒p.99)
(7) tradition(⇒p.122)

4 (1) fail／に落ちる(⇒p.98)　(2) low／低(い)(⇒p.129)
(3) quiet／静かな(⇒p.126)

復習も大事だよ！

過去問にチャレンジ！ ①

（　　）に入れるのに最も適切なものを **1**, **2**, **3**, **4** の中から一つ選びなさい。

(1) *A:* I have to write your name and (　　) on this paper. How old are you, Takeshi?
　　B: I'm 15.
　　1 age　　**2** line　　**3** air　　**4** capital
(2011-2)

(2) *A:* Jane, I (　　) my wallet. Can you lend me some money for lunch?
　　B: All right, Lucy.
　　1 put　　**2** built　　**3** spent　　**4** lost
(2011-2)

(3) *A:* Excuse me. Where is the history section?
　　B: It's on the fourth floor. You can take that (　　).
　　1 schedule　　**2** land　　**3** message　　**4** elevator
(2011-2)

(4) I don't want to go to the (　　) end of the pool because I can't swim.
　　1 deep　　**2** thirsty　　**3** heavy　　**4** natural
(2011-1)

正解 (1) **1** (⇒p.103)　(2) **4** (⇒p.53)　(3) **4** (⇒p.113)　(4) **1** (⇒p.84)

日本語訳
(1) A：この紙にあなたの名前と**年齢**を書かなければなりません。何歳ですか, タケシ？
　　B：15歳です。
(2) A：ジェーン, 財布を**なくした**の。昼食代を貸してくれない？
　　B：わかったわ, ルーシー。
(3) A：すみません。歴史のコーナーはどこですか。
　　B：4階です。あの**エレベーター**をご利用いただけます。
(4) 私は泳げないので, プールの**深い**ところに行きたくない。

でる度

A

熟語編

よくでる重要熟語 200

よくでる重要熟語(200語) ····· 138

チェックテスト ················ 163

でる度Aは，よく出題される重要熟語です。ここに掲載されている200語を覚えることで，3級の合格がぐっと近付きます。

1周目	2周目	3周目
/	/	/

0901
a few ~ [2, 3の~]

I saw him at the library **a few** minutes ago.
私は**2, 3**分前に, 彼を図書館で見かけました。

0902
a glass of ~ [コップ1杯の~]

Can I have **a glass of** milk?
牛乳を**コップ1杯**もらえますか。

0903
a little too (形容詞) [少し~すぎる]

This sweater is **a little too** big for me.
このセーターは私には**少し**大き**すぎます**。

0904
a lot [たいへん, 非常に]

He helped me **a lot** when I stayed in the U.S.
彼は私がアメリカに滞在したときに**ずいぶん**助けてくれました。

0905
a lot of ~ [多くの~]

I have **a lot of** things to do today.
今日はすることが**たくさん**あります。

0906
a pair of ~ [1組[足, 対]の~]

I want to buy **a pair of** shoes for my school trip.
私は遠足用の靴を**1足**買いたいです。

0907
a piece of ~ [1切れ[片, 枚]の~]

Would you like **a piece of** cake?
ケーキを**1切れ**いかがですか。

0908
a sheet of ~ [(紙)1枚の~]

She drew a picture on **a sheet of** paper.
彼女は**1枚**の紙に絵を描きました。

0909
a slice of ~ [（薄い）1切れの~]

He put **a slice of** lemon into his tea.
彼はレモンを**1切れ**紅茶に入れました。

0910
after a while [しばらくして]

After a while, it started to rain.
しばらくして，雨が降り始めました。

0911
after school [放課後に]

I usually go straight home **after school**.
私は，**放課後は**たいていまっすぐ帰宅します。

0912
agree with ~ [~（人）に同意する]

If you don't **agree with** me, please say so.
私**に同意し**ないのなら，どうかそう言ってください。

0913
all over the world [世界中で]

That singer is known **all over the world**.
その歌手は**世界中で**知られています。

0914
anything else [（疑問文で）ほかの何か]

Do you want me to do **anything else**, Grandma?
おばあちゃん，**ほかに何か**私にしてもらいたいことある？

0915
arrive in [at, on] ~ [~に到着する]

We will **arrive in** Chicago before noon.
正午までにはシカゴ**に着く**でしょう。

0916
as（副詞 / 形容詞）as A can [Aができるだけ~]

I'll get there **as** soon **as** I can.
できるだけ早くそちらに参ります。

熟語はできるだけ例文で覚えるようにしよう。

0917
as usual　　[いつものように]

As usual, Kate's father took a bath before dinner.
いつものように，ケイトの父親は夕食の前に入浴しました。

0918
ask (A) for ～　　[(Aに)～を求める]

We won't be able to finish the work today. Let's **ask for** help.
今日中にこの仕事を終えられそうにありませんね。助け**を求め**ましょう。

0919
ask A to do　　[A(人)に～するように頼む]

I **asked** Tony **to bring** something to drink.
私はトニーに何か飲み物**を持ってくるように頼み**ました。

0920
at first　　[最初は]

At first I didn't like math, but now it's my favorite subject.
最初，私は数学が好きではありませんでしたが，今では大好きな教科です。

0921
at last　　[ついに，とうとう]

I've finished my homework **at last**!
とうとう宿題をやり終えたぞ！

0922
at school　　[学校で]

She wants to make a lot of friends **at school**.
彼女は**学校で**たくさんの友だちを作りたいと思っています。

0923
at the end of ～　　[～の終わりに，～の突き当たりに]

We asked the teacher some questions **at the end of** the class.
私たちは授業**の終わりに**先生にいくつか質問をしました。

0924
be able to do　　[～することができる]

They made a robot that **was able to walk**.
彼らは**歩くことができる**ロボットを作りました。

0925
be absent from ~ [～を休んでいる]

Tom has **been absent from** school for three days.
トムは3日間学校**を休んでいます**。

0926
be born [生まれる]

He **was born** in the U.S., but now he lives in Canada.
彼はアメリカで**生まれました**が，今はカナダで暮らしています。

0927
be covered with ~ [～でおおわれている]

The table **was covered with** a cloth.
テーブルには布**がかかっていました**。

0928
be different from ~ [～と違う]

My idea **is different from** his.
私の考えは彼の考え**とは違います**。

0929
be famous for ~ [～で有名である]

My town **is famous for** its old castle.
私の町は古い城**で有名です**。

0930
be full of ~ [～でいっぱいである]

The sky **was full of** stars.
空は星**でいっぱいでした**。

0931
be glad to *do* [～してうれしい]

I'**m glad to know** that you've passed the exam.
あなたが試験に合格した**と知ってうれしいです**。

0932
be good at ~ [～がじょうず[得意]である]

My uncle **is good at** playing soccer.
私のおじはサッカーをするの**がじょうずです**。

〈be＋形容詞～〉の熟語をまとめて覚えよう。

0933
be in a hurry　　　　　　　　　　[急いで [あわてて] いる]

Sorry, I can't talk now. **I'm in a hurry** to get to work.
ごめんなさい，今は話せないわ。職場へ行くのに**急いでいる**の。

0934
be in trouble　　　　　　　　　　[困っている]

I'll help you when you**'re in trouble**.
あなたが**困った**ときはお手伝いします。

0935
be interested in ～　　　　　　　　　　[～に興味がある]

John **is interested in** Japanese history.
ジョンは日本の歴史に**興味をもっています**。

0936
be late for ～　　　　　　　　　　[～に遅れる]

I **was late for** school because I got up late.
私は寝坊したので学校に**遅刻しました**。

0937
be out　　　　　　　　　　[外出している]

Mr. Green **is out** right now. He'll be back by three o'clock.
グリーンさんはただ今**外出中**です。3時までには戻ります。

0938
be proud of ～　　　　　　　　　　[～を誇りに思っている]

She **is proud of** her son.
彼女は息子**を誇りに思っています**。

0939
be ready for ～　　　　　　　　　　[～の準備ができている]

I**'m ready for** the science test tomorrow.
私は明日の理科のテスト**の準備ができています**。

0940
be ready to *do*　　　　　　　　　　[～する準備ができている]

Are you **ready to** go to the party?
パーティーに出かける**準備はできていますか**。

0941
be surprised at ~ ［～に驚く］

We **were** very **surprised at** the news.
私たちはその知らせ**に**とても**驚きました**。

0942
be worried about ~ ［～を心配している］

She's **worried about** her daughter studying abroad.
彼女は海外留学中の娘**のことを心配しています**。

0943
become friends with ~ ［～と友だちになる］

I want to **become friends with** students from other countries.
私は海外から来た学生たち**と友だちになり**たいです。

0944
between *A* and *B* ［AとBの間に］

The post office is **between** a supermarket **and** a bookstore.
郵便局はスーパーと書店の**間に**あります。

0945
both *A* and *B* ［AとBの両方とも］

Both my aunt **and** I like painting.
おば**と**私は2人とも絵を描くことが好きです。

0946
both of ~ ［(2者について)～の両方とも］

I ordered pizza and a salad at that restaurant. **Both of** them were good.
私はそのレストランでピザとサラダを注文しました。**両方とも**おいしかったです。

0947
by *oneself* ［ひとりで，自分で］

Tom lives **by himself** in a small apartment.
トムは小さなアパートに**ひとりで**暮らしています。

0948
clean up ~ ［～をきれいに片づける］

Let's **clean up** the living room before dinner.
夕食の前に居間**を片づけ**ましょう。

0949
come back [戻る]

Try to finish your homework before your father **comes back**.
お父さんが**戻る**前に宿題を終わらせるようにしなさい。

0950
come home [帰宅する]

When I **came home**, my mother was cooking.
私が**帰宅した**とき，母は料理をしていました。

0951
come true [実現する]

I'm sure your dream will **come true**.
あなたの夢はきっと**かないます**よ。

0952
decide to *do* [～することに決める]

My brother **decided to buy** a used car made in Germany.
兄はドイツ製の中古車**を買うことにしました**。

0953
do *one's* best [最善を尽くす]

I'll **do my best** in the next tennis match.
次のテニスの試合では，**最善を尽くします**。

0954
do *one's* homework [宿題をする]

I usually **do my homework** before dinner.
私はたいてい夕食前に**宿題をします**。

0955
do well [うまくいく，成功する]

How was the test, Lisa? Did you **do well**?
リサ，テストはどうだった？　**よくできた**？

0956
each other [お互い]

We've known **each other** since we were small.
私たちは幼いころから**お互い**を知っています。

0957
enjoy *doing* [〜して楽しむ]

We **enjoyed watching** a football game.
私たちはフットボールの試合**を見て楽しみました**。

0958
(形容詞 / 副詞) enough for 〜 [〜に十分…]

I think this book is easy **enough for** your daughter.
この本はあなたの娘さん**には十分**やさしいと思います。

0959
(形容詞 / 副詞) enough to *do* [〜するのに十分…]

It was not hot **enough to swim** in the sea.
海で**泳ぐほどには**暑くありませんでした。

0960
exchange *A* **for** *B* [A を B と交換する]

The shirt I bought is a little too big. Could I **exchange** it **for** a smaller one? 私が買ったシャツは少し大きすぎます。小さいもの**と交換する**ことはできますか。

0961
fall down [倒れる, 転倒する]

I **fell down** when I was running to school.
学校に向かって走っていたときに**転びました**。

0962
find out 〜 [〜を見つけ出す, 〜を調べる]

Let's **find out** who stole the bag.
だれがそのかばんを盗んだのか**を見つけ出し**ましょう。

0963
finish *doing* [〜し終える]

Have you **finished washing** your shoes?
靴**を洗い終え**ましたか。

0964
first of all [まず最初に]

First of all, let me introduce myself.
まず最初に, 自己紹介をさせていただきます。

---

enjoy や finish など, あとに -ing 形が続く動詞を整理しよう。

for a long time
[長い間]

I've wanted to buy this **for a long time**.
私はこれを**長い間**買いたいと思っていました。

for example
[たとえば]

He likes European countries, **for example**, Spain and Italy.
彼はヨーロッパの国々が好きです。**たとえば**、スペインやイタリアです。

for the first time
[初めて]

Masao took a plane **for the first time** when he went to China this spring.　マサオはこの春中国に行ったときに、**初めて**飛行機に乗りました。

from A to B
[A から B まで]

She goes to swimming school **from** Monday **to** Thursday.
彼女は月曜日から木曜日まで水泳教室に通っています。

get a good grade
[よい成績をとる]

Susan likes studying and always **gets good grades**.
スーザンは勉強が好きで、いつも**よい成績をとります**。

get a perfect score
[満点をとる]

I **got a perfect score** on the math test.
数学のテストで**満点をとりました**。

get cold
[寒くなる]

It's **getting cold**. Let's go inside.
寒くなってきました。中に入りましょう。

get dark
[暗くなる]

Be back before it **gets dark**.
暗くなる前に帰ってきなさいね。

0973
get home [帰宅する]

When I **got home**, my father was washing the car.
帰宅したとき、父は車を洗っていました。

0974
get hungry [空腹になる]

Can we have lunch at that café? I'm **getting hungry**.
あのカフェで昼食をとりませんか。お腹がすいてきました。

0975
get off (〜) [(乗り物など)(を)降りる]

Let's **get off** the bus at the next stop and walk.
次の停留所でバスを降りて歩きましょう。

0976
get on (〜) [(乗り物など)(に)乗る]

Sorry I'm late. I **got on** the wrong bus.
遅れてごめんね。違うバスに乗ってしまったの。

0977
get to 〜 [〜に着く]

What time will we **get to** the airport?
私たちは何時に空港に着くでしょうか。

0978
give A a ride [A(人)を車で送る[車に乗せる]]

It was raining, so my father **gave** me **a ride** to school.
雨が降っていたので、父が私を学校まで車で送ってくれました。

0979
go and *do* [〜しに行く]

Ms. Baker, I have a stomachache. Can I **go and see** the school nurse?
ベイカー先生、おなかが痛いので、保健室の先生に診てもらいに行ってもいいですか。

0980
go back home [帰宅する]

We got very hungry, so we **went back home** for lunch.
とてもお腹がすいたので、昼食を食べに家へ帰りました。

0981

go fishing [釣りに行く]

I often **go fishing** with my father on weekends.
私は週末によく父と**釣りに行き**ます。

0982

go for a walk [散歩に行く]

I **went for a walk** in the park yesterday.
私は昨日公園に**散歩に行き**ました。

0983

go home [帰宅する]

Children, it's time to **go home**.
子どもたち，**家に帰る**時間ですよ。

0984

go on a tour [周遊旅行に出かける]

We **went on a** bus **tour** around the city.
私たちはバスで市内**周遊**をしました。

0985

go on a trip [旅行に出かける]

They **went on a trip** to Mexico.
彼らはメキシコに**旅行に行き**ました。

0986

go out (for ~) [(~のために)出かける]

It's a beautiful day. Why don't we **go out for** lunch?
天気がいいわね。ランチに**出かけ**ましょうよ。

0987

go shopping [買い物に行く]

I'm **going shopping** tomorrow. Do you want to come with me?
明日**買い物に行く**の。一緒に行かない？

0988

go [walk] straight [まっすぐに行く[歩く]]

Go straight and turn left at the next corner.
まっすぐ行って次の角で左に曲がってください。

0989
go to bed [寝る]

I have to finish my homework before I **go to bed**.
私は**寝る**前に宿題を終えなければなりません。

0990
go to see a movie [映画を見に行く]

Last weekend, I **went to see a movie** with Betty.
先週末，私はベティと**映画を見に行き**ました。

0991
go to the doctor [医師に診てもらいに行く]

I'm sorry I'm late. I had to **go to the doctor** this morning.
遅れてごめんなさい。今朝，**お医者さんに行か**なければならなかったの。

0992
go to work [仕事に行く]

Dad, do you have to **go to work** this Saturday?
お父さん，今度の土曜日は**仕事に行か**なければならないの？

0993
graduate from ~ [~を卒業する]

After **graduating from** university, she started to work as a nurse.
彼女は大学**を卒業した**後，看護師として働き始めました。

0994
grow up [大人になる, 成長する]

Tom wants to be a pilot when he **grows up**.
トムは**大きくなっ**たらパイロットになりたいと思っています。

0995
have a chance to *do* [~する機会がある]

Steve **had a chance to talk** to the writer.
スティーブはその作家と**話す機会があり**ました。

0996
have a cold [風邪をひいている]

Mom, can I stay home today? I think I **have a cold**.
お母さん，今日は家にいてもいい？ **風邪をひいてる**と思うの。

go fishing や go shopping など go -ing は「~しに行く」。

0997
have a great time [楽しく過ごす]

I'm glad to hear that you're **having a great time** in London.
私はあなたがロンドンで**楽しく過ごしている**と聞いてうれしいです。

0998
have been to ~ [~に行ったことがある]

Have you ever **been to** Australia?
これまでにオーストラリア**に行ったことがありますか**。

0999
have enough (名詞) to *do* [~するのに十分な…がある]

We don't **have enough** eggs **to make** a cake.
ケーキを作る**のに十分な**卵が**ありません**。

1000
have fun [楽しむ]

The weather was not good, but I **had fun**.
天気はよくありませんでしたが、**楽しみました**。

1001
have lunch [昼食をとる]

We **had lunch** at an Italian restaurant near the museum.
私たちは博物館近くのイタリア料理店で**昼食をとりました**。

1002
have never been to ~ [~に行ったことがない]

I'**ve never been to** Paris.
私はパリ**に行ったことがありません**。

1003
have time to *do* [~する時間がある]

We didn't **have time to visit** her last Sunday.
この前の日曜日には彼女**を訪ねる時間が**ありませんでした。

1004
have to *do* [~しなければならない]

I **have to finish** this report by next Monday.
私はこのレポートを来週の月曜日までに**終えなければなりません**。

1005
how long ~ [どのくらいの長さで~]

How long is the show?
上映は**どのくらいの長さ**ですか。

1006
how many times ~ [何回~]

How many times have you been to Hawaii?
ハワイには**何回**行ったことがありますか。

1007
how often ~ [どのくらいの頻度で~]

How often do you play tennis?
どのくらいの頻度でテニスをしますか。

1008
how to *do* [~する方法, ~の仕方]

My grandmother taught me **how to make** an apple pie.
祖母がアップルパイ**の作り方**を教えてくれました。

1009
hurry up [急ぐ]

Hurry up, or we'll be late for the concert.
急がないとコンサートに遅れちゃうよ。

1010
I'd like to *do* [~したい]

I'd like to send this package to the U.S.
この荷物をアメリカに**送りたい**のですが。

1011
in front of ~ [~の前で[に]]

Let's meet **in front of** the department store at noon.
正午にデパート**の前**で会いましょう。

1012
in *one's* opinion [~の意見では]

In my opinion, we should have another parking area near the station.
私の意見では, 駅の近くに駐車場がもう1つ必要です。

1013
in the middle of ~ [～の真ん中に，～の最中に]

Kathy fell asleep **in the middle of** the concert.
キャシーはコンサート**の最中に**眠ってしまいました。

1014
in the morning [afternoon, evening] [午前(中)[午後，夕方]に]

I studied at the library **in the morning**.
午前中に，私は図書館で勉強しました。

1015
in the world [世界で]

Mt. Everest is the highest mountain **in the world**.
エベレスト山は**世界で**最も高い山です。

1016
invite A to B [A(人)をBに招待する]

Nancy **invited** us **to** her birthday party.
ナンシーは私たち**を**誕生日パーティー**に招待**してくれました。

1017
It is (形容詞) for A to do [A(人)が～するのは…だ]

It is difficult **for** me **to finish** the report today.
今日中にレポートを仕上げる**のは**私に**は**難しい**のです**。

1018
It takes A (時間) to do [A(人)が～するのに(時間)がかかる]

It took me a month **to read** the book.
その本**を読むのに**1か月**かかりました**。

1019
last week [month, year] [先週[先月，昨年]]

I went skiing with my friend **last week**.
先週，私は友だちとスキーに行きました。

1020
laugh at ~ [～を聞いて[見て]笑う]

Everyone **laughed at** his funny story.
みんなが彼のこっけいな話**を聞いて笑いました**。

1021
leave *A* at home
[A を家に置き忘れる]

I **left** my wallet **at home**.
私は家に財布を置いてきてしまいました。

1022
leave a message
[伝言を残す]

Sorry, but she is out now. Would you like to **leave a message**?
申し訳ありませんが，彼女は今，外出中です。伝言はございますか。

1023
look around (〜)
[辺りを見回す，〜を見て回る]

I didn't have enough time to **look around** the town.
町を見て回る時間が十分にありませんでした。

1024
look for 〜
[〜を探す]

We went out to **look for** the lost dog.
私たちは迷子の犬を探しに出かけました。

1025
look forward to *doing* [*A*]
[〜するのを [A を] 楽しみに待つ]

I'm **looking forward to seeing** you again.
またあなたに会えるのを楽しみにしています。

1026
look well
[元気そうに見える]

What's the matter? You don't **look well**.
どうしたの？ 具合がよくなさそうだね。

1027
lots of 〜
[多くの〜]

You don't have to bring anything. There will be **lots of** food.
何も持ってこなくていいですよ。食べるものはたくさんあります。

1028
make a speech
[スピーチ [演説] をする]

Gordon had to **make a** long **speech** at a meeting yesterday.
ゴードンは昨日の会合で長いスピーチをしなければなりませんでした。

---

look well の well は「元気な」という意味の形容詞だよ。

1029
more than ~ ［〜より多い］

There were **more than** 100 people at the party.
そのパーティーには 100 人を**超える**人がいました。

1030
most of ~ ［〜のほとんど］

Most of the students go to school by bus.
生徒**のほとんど**がバスで学校へ行きます。

1031
move to ~ ［〜に引っ越す，〜に移動する］

The office **moved to** a different floor.
オフィスは違う階**に移動しました**。

1032
near here ［この近くに］

Are there any good restaurants **near here**?
この近くによいレストランはありますか。

1033
need to *do* ［〜する必要がある］

We **need to find** someone who can speak French.
私たちはフランス語が話せる人を見つける**必要があります**。

1034
not ~ at all ［まったく〜ない］

I did**n't** understand what Mike said **at all**.
私はマイクの言うことが**まったく**理解でき**ません**でした。

1035
not ~ yet ［まだ〜ない］

I have**n't** finished cleaning my room **yet**.
私は**まだ**部屋の掃除を終えてい**ません**。

1036
not have to *do* ［〜しなくてよい］

You do**n't have to eat** everything.
全部**食べなくていい**んだよ。

1037
not only *A* but also *B* [AだけでなくBも]

Not only Cathy **but also** her sister can dance very well.
キャシー**だけでなく**彼女の妹**も**とてもダンスがじょうずです。

1038
on business [仕事で]

Linda's father sometimes goes to Los Angeles **on business**.
リンダの父親はときどき**仕事で**ロサンゼルスへ行きます。

1039
on *one's* [the] right [右手に]

Turn left at that flower shop, and you'll see it **on your right**.
あの花屋を左に曲がるとそれが**右手に**見えますよ。

1040
on *one's* [the] way home [家に帰る途中で]

I'll get something for dinner **on my way home**.
家に帰る途中で夕食に何か買うよ。

1041
on *one's* [the] way to ～ [～へ行く途中で]

Jason often buys coffee **on his way to** work.
ジェイソンはよく仕事**へ行く途中で**コーヒーを買います。

1042
on weekends [週末に]

What do you usually do **on weekends**?
週末にはたいてい何をしますか。

1043
one more (名詞) [もう1人[1つ]の～]

I think we need **one more** volunteer.
私たちにはボランティアが**もう1人**必要だと思います。

1044
one of ～ [～の1人[1つ]]

They have three children. **One of** them is a college student.
彼らには3人の子どもがいます。そのうち**の1人**は大学生です。

1045
one of the＋(形容詞の最上級)＋(複数名詞)　[最も～な…の１つ]

Boston is **one of the** oldest cities in the U.S.
ボストンはアメリカで**最も**古い都市**の１つ**です。

1046
over there　[向こうで[に]]

Who is the girl playing tennis **over there**?
向こうでテニスをしている女の子はだれですか。

1047
pass the [an] exam　[試験に合格する]

Study hard, and you'll **pass the exam**.
一生懸命に勉強すれば**試験に合格する**でしょう。

1048
pick up ～　[～を車で迎えに来る[行く]]

Hello, Mom? It's raining. Could you **pick** me **up** at the station?
もしもし，お母さん？　雨が降っているの。駅に**車で迎えに来て**くれない？

1049
put on ～　[～を着る]

It was cold, so I **put on** a coat.
寒かったのでコートを**着ました**。

1050
receive a prize　[賞を受ける]

She **received** the first **prize** in the contest.
彼女はそのコンテストで１**等賞を取りました**。

1051
right now　[ちょうど今，すぐに]

I'm afraid she can't get to the phone **right now**.
あいにく彼女は**ただ今**電話に出ることができません。

1052
run away　[逃げ去る，走り去る]

The news says that a lion **ran away** from the zoo.
ニュースによると，１頭のライオンが動物園から**逃げ出しました**。

1053
save money [貯金する]

Jane is working after school to **save money**.
ジェーンは**お金を貯める**ため，放課後に働いています。

1054
say hello to ~ [~によろしく伝える]

I can't go with you. Please **say hello to** Grandma for me.
私は一緒に行けないわ。おばあちゃん**によろしく伝えて**ね。

1055
shake hands with ~ [~と握手する]

You can **shake hands with** the members of the band over there.
向こうでバンドのメンバー**と握手する**ことができます。

1056
shout at ~ [~に叫ぶ]

He **shouted at** his son, "Watch out! A car is coming."
彼は息子に「危ない！ 車が来ているよ」と**叫びました**。

1057
show A how to do [A (人) に~のやり方を教える]

Can you **show** me **how to use** this machine?
この機械**の使い方を教え**てくれますか。

1058
so (形容詞/副詞) that ~ [とても…なので~]

We were **so** tired **that** we went to bed early.
私たちは**非常に**疲れていた**ので**，早く寝ました。

1059
something (形容詞) [何か~なもの]

Let's make **something** special for dinner.
夕食に**何か**特別**なもの**を作りましょう。

1060
something to do [何か~する [すべき] もの]

I want to get **something to read** on the train.
何か電車の中で**読むもの**を買いたいです。

(代名詞 (-thing など)) + (形容詞) の語順も確認しよう。

1061
spend *A* on ～ [A（時間・お金）を～に費やす]

Mr. Smith **spends** a lot of money **on** books.
スミス氏は本に多くのお金**を使います**。

1062
stay home [家にいる]

I have to **stay home** and take care of my little sister.
私は**家にいて**妹の面倒をみなければなりません。

1063
stay up late [夜更かしする]

I'm sleepy because I **stayed up late** last night.
昨夜**夜更かしした**ので眠いです。

1064
such a [an]（形容詞）（名詞） [そのような～]

I've never had **such a** delicious cake.
こんなおいしいケーキは食べたことがありません。

1065
take *A* to *B* [AをBに連れていく]

Dad **took** me **to** the baseball game.
父さんはぼく**を**その野球の試合**に連れていって**くれました。

1066
take a picture [写真を撮る]

Jenny **took** a lot of **pictures** during her trip.
ジェニーは旅行中に**写真を**たくさん**撮りました**。

1067
take care of ～ [～の世話をする]

Who's going to **take care of** your dog while you're on vacation?
休暇中はだれが君の犬**の世話をする**のですか。

1068
take lessons [レッスンを受ける]

Laura **takes** piano **lessons** because she wants to be a pianist.
ローラはピアニストになりたいのでピアノの**レッスンを受けている**。

1069
take off
[離陸する]

Our plane **took off** on time.
私たちの飛行機は定刻に**離陸しました**。

1070
take off ~
[～を脱ぐ]

He **took off** his hat and greeted the teacher.
彼は帽子**を脱いで**先生にあいさつをしました。

1071
take part in ~
[～に参加する]

Lisa is going to **take part in** the speech contest next month.
リサは来月スピーチコンテスト**に参加する**つもりです。

1072
talk on the phone
[電話で話す]

Do you know that man **talking on the phone**?
電話で話しているあの男性を知っていますか。

1073
tell *A* how to *do*
[A（人）に～のやり方を教える]

Could you **tell** me **how to get** to the museum?
博物館への**行き方を教えて**いただけませんか。

1074
tell *A* to *do*
[A（人）に～するように言う]

My mother often **tells** me **to read** books.
母はよく私に本**を読むように言います**。

1075
than usual
[いつもより]

Makoto got up earlier **than usual** to do his homework.
マコトは宿題をするために**いつもより**早く起きました。

1076
the other day
[先日]

I met an old friend of mine on the street **the other day**.
先日、私は通りで昔の友だちに会いました。

1077
think about *doing* [〜することについて考える]

I'm **thinking about doing** a part-time job.
アルバイトをしようと考えています。

1078
think of ~ [〜のことを考える]

What do you **think of** his opinion?
彼の意見を**どう思います**か。

1079
this morning [今朝]

It was raining **this morning**, but it's sunny now.
今朝は雨が降っていましたが，今は晴れています。

1080
throw away ~ [〜を捨てる]

Don't **throw away** these magazines. I need them for my report.
これらの雑誌**は捨て**ないでください。レポートに必要なのです。

1081
too (形容詞 / 副詞) to *do* [とても…なので〜できない]

Paul was **too** busy **to go** to Ms. Brown's farewell party.
ポールは**あまりに**忙しかった**ので**ブラウン先生のお別れ会に**行けません**でした。

1082
travel to ~ [〜へ旅行する]

He **traveled to** Seattle by train.
彼は列車でシアトル**へ旅行しました**。

1083
try on ~ [〜を試着する]

I like this hat. May I **try** it **on**?
この帽子が気に入っています。**試着して**もよろしいですか。

1084
turn down ~ [（テレビやラジオなど）の音量を下げる]

Could you **turn down** the music? I'm studying.
音楽**の音量を下げて**くれませんか。勉強しているのです。

1085
turn left [right] [左[右]に曲がる]

Turn left at the second traffic light.
2つ目の信号で**左に曲がって**ください。

1086
turn off ~ [(水道・ガス・明かりなど)を消す[止める]]

Turn off the light when you leave the room.
部屋を出るときには，明かり**を消して**ください。

1087
turn on ~ [(水道・ガス・明かりなど)をつける[出す]]

It's cold here. Shall we **turn on** the heater?
ここは寒いですね。暖房**をつけ**ましょうか。

1088
turn up ~ [(テレビやラジオなど)の音量を上げる]

I can't hear the radio well. Can you **turn** it **up**?
ラジオがよく聞こえません。**音量を上げて**くれますか。

1089
twice a month [week, day] [月[週, 日]に2回]

I work at the hospital as a volunteer **twice a month**.
私は**月に2回**，ボランティアとして病院で働いています。

1090
visit [see] *A* in the hospital [入院中のA(人)を見舞う]

I **visited** my friend **in the hospital**.
私は**入院中の友人**を見舞いに行きました。

1091
wait for ~ [~を待つ]

I'll **wait for** you in the gym.
体育館であなた**を待って**います。

1092
wake up [起きる, 目が覚める]

Lucy **woke up** early today.
ルーシーは今日早く**起きた**。

---

think about *doing* など前置詞のあとの動詞は -ing 形。

1093
walk along ~ [～に沿って歩く]

I **walking along** the river in spring.
私は春に川沿いを歩くのが好きです。

1094
want A to do [A(人)に～してもらいたい]

My father **wants** me **to become** a doctor.
父はぼくに医者になってほしいと思っています。

1095
want to be [become] [～になりたい]

I **want to be** an astronaut in the future.
ぼくは将来，宇宙飛行士になりたいです。

1096
what to do [何を～すべきか]

I don't know **what to wear** for the school trip.
遠足に何を着ていけばよいかわかりません。

1097
when to do [いつ～すべきか]

We talked about **when to hold** the welcome party for Mr. Scott.
私たちはスコットさんの歓迎会をいつ開くべきか話し合いました。

1098
where to do [どこへ[で]～すべきか]

The summer vacation starts next week, but we haven't decided **where to go** yet.　来週から夏休みが始まりますが，どこへ行くかまだ決めていません。

1099
work well [うまくいく]

The plan **worked** very **well**.
その計画はとてもうまくいきました。

1100
~ year(s) old [～歳]

I visited China when I was ten **years old**.
私は10歳のときに中国を訪れました。

熟語編 でる度 A

チェックテスト

1 下線の語句の意味を①〜③の中から選びましょう。

(1) **look for** my cat
① 〜を探す　② 〜を心配している　③ 〜を見つけ出す

(2) when I **grow up**
① 成長する　② 帰宅する　③ 倒れる

(3) **in the middle of** July
① 〜の初めに　② 〜の真ん中に　③ 〜の終わりに

(4) The dream **came true**.
① 思い出した　② やって来た　③ 実現した

2 日本語に合うように（　）に適切な語を下の①〜⑥の中から選びましょう。

(1) 私は彼を誇りに思っている。　I'm (　　) of him.

(2) 彼女は泳ぐことができる。　She is (　　) to swim.

(3) 彼は料理がじょうずだ。　He is (　　) at cooking.

(4) 私は学校に遅刻した。　I was (　　) for school.

(5) 試験の準備はできていますか。
Are you (　　) for the exam?

① able	② absent	③ ready
④ good	⑤ proud	⑥ late

お疲れさま！ 「でる度 A」はこれで終わりだよ。

3 日本語に合うように（　）に英単語を入れましょう。

(1) 夜更かしする　　stay (　　　　　　) late

(2) ラジオを消す　　(　　　　　　　　) off the radio

(3) 彼は英語だけでなくスペイン語も話す。
He speaks not only English (　　　　　　) also Spanish.

(4) 最初は，私は数学が好きではなかった。
(　　　　　　) first, I didn't like math.

4 日本語に合うように①～③の中から選びましょう。

(1) 一切れのケーキ　　a (① sheet　② piece　③ pair) of cake

(2) 2, 3 日前に　　a (① little　② lot　③ few) days ago

(3) 飛行機が離陸した。
A plane (① turned　② took　③ got) off.

5 (　) に入る語を右の①～④の中から選びましょう。

(1) The mountain is covered (　　) snow.

(2) I'll help you when you are (　　) trouble.

(3) We went (　　) a trip to Canada.

(4) I couldn't understand the story (　　) all.

① on
② in
③ at
④ with

正解

3 (1) up (⇒p.158)　(2) turn (⇒p.161)　(3) but (⇒p.155)
　　(4) At (⇒p.140)

4 (1) ② (⇒p.138)　(2) ③ (⇒p.138)　(3) ② (⇒p.159)

5 (1) ④ (⇒p.141)　(2) ② (⇒p.142)　(3) ① (⇒p.148)　(4) ③ (⇒p.154)

でる度 A

B

熟語編

差がつく応用熟語 200

差がつく応用熟語 (200語) …… 166

チェックテスト …… 192

過去問にチャレンジ！② …… 194

でる度 B は，試験に出る頻度は下がりますが，いざというときに差がつく熟語です。ここに掲載されている 200 語を覚えれば，3 級レベルの語彙はばっちりです。

1周目	2周目	3周目
/	/	/

1101

a couple of ~ [2つ[2人]の~, 2, 3の~]

I'm going to stay in Oxford for **a couple of** weeks.
私は**2, 3**週間オックスフォードに滞在するつもりです。

1102

a friend of mine [私の友だちの1人]

I went cycling with **a friend of mine**.
私は**友だちの1人**とサイクリングに行きました。

1103

a number of ~ [多くの~, 多数の~]

A number of people were saved from the burning building.
たくさんの人が燃えるビルから救助された。

1104

(a) part of ~ [~の一部]

Cleaning these rooms is **part of** his job.
これらの部屋を掃除することは彼の仕事**の一部**です。

1105

all day (long) [一日中]

It will be sunny **all day** tomorrow.
明日は**一日中**晴れるでしょう。

1106

all night (long) [一晩中]

I studied for the exam **all night**.
私は**一晩中**試験勉強をしました。

1107

all the time [常に, いつでも]

He never listens. He just talks **all the time**.
彼は決して人の話を聞かない。**いつも**しゃべってばかりだ。

1108

all the way [はるばる, ずっと]

He had to walk **all the way** home from school.
彼は学校から家まで**ずっと**歩かなければなりませんでした。

1109
~ and so on [〜など]

He took her to the Statue of Liberty, Broadway, **and so on**.
彼は彼女を自由の女神像，ブロードウェイ**など**に連れていきました。

1110
another (形容詞) minute(s) [あと〜分]

Could you give me **another** ten **minutes**?
あと 10 **分**待ってもらえますか。

1111
as many (名詞) as ~ [〜ほどたくさんの…]

I don't have **as many** books **as** you.
私はあなた**ほどたくさんの**本を持っていません。

1112
as much as A can [Aができるだけ(たくさん)]

I want to learn **as much as** I **can** during my homestay in Canada.
カナダでのホームステイの間に**できるだけ**多く学びたいと思います。

1113
as much as possible [できるだけ(たくさん)]

Naomi tried to speak English **as much as possible**.
ナオミは**できるだけ**英語を話そうと試みました。

1114
as soon as ~ [〜するとすぐに]

Please call me **as soon as** you get home.
家に着い**たらすぐに**私に電話をください。

1115
A as well as B [Bと同様にAも]

They grow fruit **as well as** vegetables.
彼らは野菜だけでなく果物**も**栽培しています。

1116
as you know [ご存じのように]

As you know, ice hockey is a very popular sport in Canada.
ご存じのように，アイスホッケーはカナダでとても人気のあるスポーツです。

many のあとは数えられる名詞が続くよ。

1117

at a time [一度に]

It's difficult to listen to five different people **at a time**.
一度に5人の言うことに耳を傾けるのは困難です。

1118

at least [少なくとも]

I have **at least** a hundred CDs.
私は**少なくとも**100枚のCDを持っています。

1119

at once [すぐに]

When Mr. Jones opened the door, the students stopped talking **at once**. ジョーンズ先生がドアを開けると、生徒たちは**すぐに**話すのをやめました。

1120

at the age of ～ [～歳のときに]

Our teacher went to America **at the age of** twenty-three.
私たちの先生は23**歳のときに**アメリカに行きました。

1121

at the foot of ～ [～のふもとに]

Her town is **at the foot of** a mountain.
彼女の町は山**のふもとに**あります。

1122

be afraid of ～ [～を恐れる]

Don't **be afraid of** making mistakes.
間違えること**を恐れて**はいけません。

1123

be at home [家にいる]

Will you **be at home** this evening?
あなたは今晩、**家にいます**か。

1124

be at *one's* desk [机に向かっている，席についている]

I'm afraid she's not **at her desk** right now.
あいにく彼女はただ今**席におりません**。

1125
be back [戻る]

Mom, I'm going out now, but I'll **be back** before dinner.
お母さん，今から外出するけど，夕食までには**戻る**ね。

1126
be busy with ~ [～で忙しい]

My father **is busy with** his work.
私の父は仕事**で忙しい**です。

1127
be careful (about ~) [(～に)気をつける]

I think you should **be** more **careful about** your health.
あなたはもっと健康**に気をつけた**方がいいと思います。

1128
be close to ~ [～に近い]

His house **is close to** the river, so he often goes swimming there.
彼の家は川**の近くにある**ので，彼はよくそこに泳ぎに行きます。

1129
be familiar with ~ [～をよく知っている]

I **was** not **familiar with** the city, so I didn't know where to go.
私はその街**をよく知らなかった**ので，どこに行けばよいかわかりませんでした。

1130
be filled with ~ [～でいっぱいである]

The hall **was filled with** young people.
そのホールは若者**でいっぱいでした**。

1131
be fond of ~ [～が好きだ，～を好む]

She **is fond of** traveling.
彼女は旅行をするの**が好きです**。

1132
be known as ~ [～として知られている]

Chicago **is known as** "the Windy City."
シカゴは「風の(強い)都市」**として知られています**。

1133
be known to ~ [〜に知られている]

That singer **is known to** people all over the world.
あの歌手は世界中の人々に**知られています**。

1134
be over [終わる]

The game **was over** when George arrived.
ジョージが到着したとき，試合は**終わっていました**。

1135
be pleased to *do* [〜してうれしい]

I'm **pleased to meet** you.
あなたにお会いできて**うれしく思います**。

1136
be satisfied with ~ [〜に満足している]

I'm **satisfied with** their service.
私は彼らのサービス**に満足**です。

1137
be scared of ~ [〜を恐れる，〜が怖い]

Emily can't swim in a pool because she**'s scared of** water.
エミリーは水**が怖い**のでプールで泳ぐことができません。

1138
be sick in bed [病気で寝ている]

Mary has **been sick in bed** for ten days.
メアリーは10日間**病気で寝ています**。

1139
be similar to ~ [〜に似ている]

His way of thinking **is similar to** yours.
彼の考え方はあなたの考え方**と似ています**。

1140
be sorry for *doing* [〜して申し訳なく思う]

I'm very **sorry for breaking** my promise.
約束**を破ってしまって**本当にごめんなさい。

1141
be surprised to *do* ［～して驚く］

I **was surprised to see** so many people at the festival.
私はそのお祭りでとても多くの人を見て驚きました。

1142
be tired from ～ ［～で疲れている］

He went to bed earlier because he **was tired from** traveling.
彼は旅行で疲れていたので，早めに寝ました。

1143
be tired of *doing* ［～することに飽きる［うんざりする］］

I'm **tired of watching** TV. Let's go for a walk.
テレビを見るのに飽きました。散歩に行きましょう。

1144
because of ～ ［～のために］

We didn't go to see the soccer game **because of** bad weather.
悪天候のためサッカーの試合を見に行きませんでした。

1145
belong to ～ ［～に属する］

I **belong to** the photography club at school.
私は学校で写真部に所属しています。

1146
brush *one's* teeth ［歯をみがく］

Sam, **brush your teeth** before going to bed.
サム，寝る前に歯をみがきなさい。

1147
by the way ［ところで］

By the way, how was your trip to New Zealand?
ところで，ニュージーランドへの旅行はいかがでしたか。

1148
call *A* back ［A(人)に折り返し電話する］

I'm afraid she is out. Do you want her to **call you back**?
あいにく彼女は外出しています。折り返し電話をかけさせましょうか。

---

be surprised to *do* は不定詞の「～して…」という用法だよ。

1149

care about ~ [～を気づかう]

If you **care about** your health, why don't you exercise?
健康を**気づかう**なら、運動してはどうですか。

1150

catch a cold [風邪をひく]

He **caught a cold** and couldn't go on the school trip.
彼は**風邪をひいて**遠足に行けませんでした。

1151

change trains [電車を乗り換える]

Get off at Central Park and **change trains** there.
セントラルパーク駅で降りて、**電車を乗り換えて**ください。

1152

cheer up ~ [～を元気づける]

Let's try to **cheer up** Naomi.
ナオミを**元気づけ**よう。

1153

cut down ~ [～を切り倒す]

If you **cut down** that tree, you will get more light in winter.
あの木を**切り倒せ**ば、冬にもっと光が当たるでしょう。

1154

day after day [くる日もくる日も、毎日]

Day after day, he wears the same jacket.
毎日、彼は同じジャケットを着ています。

1155

day and night [昼も夜も]

The work continues **day and night**.
その作業は**日夜**続きます。

1156

depend on ~ [～次第である]

It **depends on** the weather. If it's sunny, I'll go fishing.
天気**次第**です。晴れたら釣りに行きます。

1157
die of ~ [～で死ぬ]

She **died of** old age at the age of 90.
彼女は90歳で、老衰で**亡くなりました**。

1158
drive A home [A(人)を車で家まで送る]

It's getting dark. Shall I **drive** you **home**?
暗くなってきたよ。**家まで車で送って**いこうか。

1159
either A or B [AかBのどちらか]

Either you **or** Bob must do it.
君かボブ**のどちらか**がそれをしなければなりません。

1160
enjoy *oneself* [楽しむ, 楽しく過ごす]

I hope you will **enjoy yourself** at the party.
あなたがパーティーで**楽しく過ごす**ことを望んでいます。

1161
even if ~ [たとえ～でも]

She ran every morning **even if** it rained.
たとえ雨が降っ**ても**彼女は毎朝走りました。

1162
every other day [1日おきに]

Mike goes to the gym **every other day**.
マイクは**1日おきに**ジムに行きます。

1163
fall asleep [眠りに落ちる]

Today he was so tired that he **fell asleep** during class.
今日彼はとても疲れていたので、授業中に**眠ってしまいました**。

1164
fall in love with ~ [～に恋をする]

Nancy **fell in love with** one of her classmates.
ナンシーは同級生の1人**に恋をしました**。

far away　　　　　　　　　　　　　　　　[遠くに]

My father usually drives me to school because I live **far away**.
遠くに住んでいるので，いつも父が学校まで車で送ってくれます。

far from ~　　　　　　　　　　　　　　[~から遠い]

Is your house **far from** the station?
あなたの家は駅**から遠い**ですか。

feel at home　　　　　　　　　　　　　　[くつろぐ]

She **feels at home** in Canada.
彼女はカナダに来ると**くつろいだ**気分になります。

feel better　　　　　[体調がよくなる，気分がよくなる]

I had a fever this morning, but now I'm **feeling better**.
今朝は熱がありましたが，今は**気分がよくなりました**。

feel like *doing*　　　　　　　　　　[~したい気がする]

I don't **feel like going** to see a movie tonight.
今夜は映画を見に**行きたい気分**ではありません。

feel sick　　　　　　　　　　　　　　　[気分が悪い]

I have a headache and **feel sick**.
頭痛がして**気分が悪い**です。

fill in ~　　　　　　　　　　　　　[~に[を]記入する]

Please **fill in** the blanks.
空所**に記入して**ください。

fill up (with~)　　　　　　　　　[(~で)いっぱいになる]

The room **filled up with** desks and chairs.
その部屋は机といす**でいっぱいになりました**。

1173
for a minute [少しの間, 一瞬]

Helen, can you come here **for a minute**?
ヘレン，**ちょっと**ここに来てくれますか。

1174
for a while [しばらくの間]

She went to the cafeteria to rest **for a while**.
彼女は**しばらく**休憩しにカフェテリアに行きました。

1175
for fun [楽しみで]

Jeff is learning painting **for fun**.
ジェフは**楽しみで**絵画を習っています。

1176
for *oneself* [自分のために, 自分で]

Kevin sometimes cooks **for himself**.
ケビンはときどき**自分で**料理を作ります。

1177
for some time [しばらく[少し]の間]

I haven't seen her **for some time**.
私は**しばらく**彼女に会っていません。

1178
forget to *do* [〜することを忘れる]

Don't **forget to mail** this letter on your way to school.
学校に行く途中で，この手紙**を投函するのを忘れ**ないでください。

1179
from abroad [海外から(の)]

Volunteers will help people **from abroad** at the event.
その催しでは，ボランティアが**海外から**来た人たちを手伝います。

1180
from beginning to end [始めから終わりまで]

I read the whole book **from beginning to end** in one day.
私はその本を1日で**始めから終わりまで**全部読みました。

「〜から遠い」は a long way from 〜 とも言うよ。

1181
get angry [怒る]
She **got angry** because I broke her favorite cup.
私が彼女のお気に入りのカップを割ったので，彼女は**怒り**ました。

1182
get away from ~ [~から離れる[逃げる]]
He often **gets away from** the city for a rest.
彼はよく休息のために街**を離れ**ます。

1183
get back (from ~) [(~から)戻る]
I **got back from** the trip yesterday morning.
昨日の朝，旅行**から戻り**ました。

1184
get better [じょうずになる，上達する]
My Spanish **got better** during my stay in Spain.
スペイン滞在中に，私のスペイン語は**上達し**ました。

1185
get excited [興奮する]
The fans **got excited** when the singer came on stage.
その歌手が舞台に登場すると，ファンたちは**興奮し**ました。

1186
get in ~ [~に入る，~に乗りこむ]
The man told him to **get in** the car.
その男性は彼に車**に乗る**ように言いました。

1187
get out of ~ [~から出る]
She wanted him to **get out of** her room.
彼女は彼に部屋**から出て**行ってもらいたいと思いました。

1188
get well [健康になる，(病気が)治る]
I hope she'll **get well** soon.
彼女がすぐに**よくなる**ことを願っています。

1189
give back ~ [～を返す]

Will you **give back** my dictionary? I need it tomorrow.
私の辞書を**返して**くれますか。明日それが必要なのです。

1190
give up *doing* [～することをやめる，あきらめる]

My father **gave up smoking** twenty years ago.
父は20年前に**たばこをやめました**。

1191
go abroad [海外に行く]

My uncle often **goes abroad** for work.
私のおじは仕事でよく**海外へ行きます**。

1192
go away [立ち去る，(痛み，問題などが)なくなる]

I took some medicine a few hours ago, but my headache hasn't **gone away**.　数時間前に薬を飲みましたが，頭痛が**治りません**。

1193
go by [(時が)過ぎ去る]

A few weeks **went by**, and the boy's bike was found near the park.
数週間が**過ぎ**，その少年の自転車は公園の近くで見つかりました。

1194
go into ~ [～に入る]

Please take off your shoes when you **go into** the house.
家**に入る**ときは靴を脱いでください。

1195
go to sleep [寝る]

You must brush your teeth before you **go to sleep**.
寝る前に歯を磨かなければいけないよ。

1196
had better *do* [～した方がよい]

You**'d better get** the ticket right now.
すぐにチケット**を入手した方がいい**ですよ。

疲れてきたら，休憩も大事だよ。

1197
happen to *do* [たまたま～する，偶然～する]

I **happened to meet** him while I was in New York City.
私はニューヨーク市にいるとき，たまたま彼に会いました。

1198
have a baby [赤ちゃんを産む]

My aunt is going to **have a baby** next month.
来月おばは**赤ちゃんを産む**予定です。

1199
have a dream [夢を持つ]

It is important for you to **have a dream** for the future.
将来の**夢を持つ**ことは大切です。

1200
have a fight [けんかをする]

Yesterday, Eric and Frank **had a fight** at school.
昨日，エリックとフランクは学校で**けんかをしました**。

1201
have a good memory [記憶力がいい]

She **has a good memory**. She remembers almost everything about me.
彼女は**記憶力がいい**。私についてほとんどすべてのことを覚えています。

1202
have a good sleep [ぐっすり眠る]

I **had a good sleep** last night.
昨夜私は**ぐっすり眠りました**。

1203
have a stomachache [腹痛がする]

Kate was absent from school yesterday because she **had a stomachache**. ケイトは昨日**腹痛がした**ので学校を休みました。

1204
have a talk [話をする]

The teacher wants to **have a talk** with Ken's parents.
先生はケンの両親と**話をし**たがっています。

1205
have no idea
[わからない]

I **have no idea** what to get for her birthday.
彼女の誕生日に何を買ったらいいか**わかりません**。

1206
hear from ~
[～から便りがある]

I haven't **heard from** my brother since February.
2月以来，兄**から便りがありません**。

1207
hear of ~
[～を耳にする]

Have you **heard of** the new city plan?
新しい都市計画**のことを聞いた**ことがありますか。

1208
help *A* with ~
[A(人)の～を手伝う]

Paul often **helps** his father **with** his work.
ポールはよく父親の仕事**を手伝います**。

1209
how far ~
[どのくらいの距離で～]

How far is it from here to the station?
ここから駅まで**どのくらいの距離**ですか。

1210
hundreds of ~
[何百もの～，たくさんの～]

Hundreds of people were waiting outside the TV studio.
テレビスタジオの外では**何百人もの**人が待っていました。

1211
in a circle
[輪になって]

The children sat **in a circle** and sang a song.
子どもたちは**輪になって**座り，歌を歌いました。

1212
in a group
[グループ[団体]で]

Students talked about the topic **in a group**.
生徒たちは**グループで**その話題について話し合いました。

hundreds [thousands] of ~の形では s がつくよ。

1213
in a minute [すぐに]

I'll be back **in a minute**.
すぐに戻ります。

1214
in fact [実は, それどころかむしろ]

Bill is very good at soccer. **In fact**, he's the best player in the school.
ビルはサッカーがとてもじょうずです。**実際**, 彼は学校で一番じょうずな選手です。

1215
in peace [静かに, 平和に]

Tell the children to play outside. I want to read the newspaper **in peace**. 子どもたちに外で遊ぶように言ってくれ。**静かに**新聞が読みたいんだ。

1216
in public [公に, 人前で]

She is too shy to speak **in public**.
彼女はとても内気で**人前で**話すことができません。

1217
in return [お返しに]

She gave me a wallet and I gave her a scarf **in return**.
彼女は私に財布をくれました。私は**お返しに**彼女にスカーフをあげました。

1218
in spite of ~ [~にもかかわらず]

We decided to go out **in spite of** the bad weather.
悪天候**にもかかわらず**, 私たちは外出することにしました。

1219
in the end [最後に, 結局]

In the end, he decided to go to college.
結局, 彼は大学に進学することにしました。

1220
in those days [その当時は]

In those days, there was no TV.
その当時は, テレビはありませんでした。

1221
in time (for ~) [（～に）間に合って]

Beth ran as fast as she could and was **in time for** the train.
ベスはできるだけ速く走って，電車に**間に合いました**。

1222
instead of ~ [～の代わりに]

We ordered green salad **instead of** onion soup.
私たちはオニオンスープ**の代わりに**グリーンサラダを注文しました。

1223
introduce A to B [A（人）をB（人）に紹介する]

First, let me **introduce** my friend Ben **to** all of you.
最初に，私の友人のベン**を**みんな**に紹介させてください**。

1224
keep in touch with ~ [～と連絡を保つ]

I still **keep in touch with** James by e-mail.
私は今でもEメールでジェームズ**と連絡をとっています**。

1225
keep one's promise [約束を守る]

Andy always **keeps his promise**.
アンディはいつも**約束を守ります**。

1226
lie down [横になる]

I was very tired, so I **lay down** for a while.
私はとても疲れていたので，しばらく**横になりました**。

1227
like this [このように]

You can switch on the computer **like this**.
こんなふうにコンピューターのスイッチを入れるんだよ。

1228
little by little [少しずつ]

The Earth is getting warmer **little by little**.
地球は**少しずつ**暖かくなっています。

look after ~ [〜の世話をする]

Could you **look after** my daughter while I go to the post office?
郵便局へ行っている間,娘の**面倒をみて**もらえますか。

look like ~ [〜のように見える,〜に似ている]

It **looks like** the dress I want.
それは私がほしいドレス**に似ています**。

look out of ~ [〜から外を見る]

Mary **looked out of** the window and found it was snowing.
メアリーは窓**から外を見ると**,雪が降っていることに気づきました。

look up ~ [(辞書で単語など)を調べる]

Look up the word in your dictionary.
その単語を辞書で**調べ**なさい。

lose *one's* way [道に迷う]

Excuse me. I've **lost my way**. Where are we on this map?
すみません,**道に迷いました**。ここはこの地図でどこですか。

make *A* from *B* [B(原料・材料)でAを作る]

Wine is **made from** grapes.
ワインはブドウ**から作られ**ます。

make *A* into *B* [(加工して)AでBを作る]

They **make** cacao beans **into** chocolate at this factory.
この工場で,彼らはカカオ豆でチョコレート**を作り**ます。

make *A* of *B* [B(原料・材料)でAを作る]

We bought two chairs that were **made of** wood.
私たちは木**で作られた**いすを2脚買いました。

1237
make a mistake　　　[間違える]

I **made** a few **mistakes** on my English writing test.
私は英作文のテストで少し**間違えました**。

1238
make (a) noise　　　[音を立てる, 騒ぐ]

Be quiet! You're **making** too much **noise**.
静かにしなさい！ **騒ぎ**すぎですよ。

1239
make money　　　[お金をもうける, かせぐ]

He worked very hard and **made** a lot of **money**.
彼はとても熱心に働き, たくさんの**お金をもうけました**。

1240
name *A* after *B*　　　[BにちなんでAに名前をつける]

The baby was **named after** his grandfather.
その赤ちゃんはおじいさん**にちなんで命名**されました。

1241
neither *A* nor *B*　　　[AもBも〜ない]

He can speak **neither** Japanese **nor** Chinese.
彼は日本語も中国語も話せません。

1242
next door　　　[隣に]

The woman who lives **next door** is a doctor.
隣に住んでいる女性は医者です。

1243
next time　　　[次回(は)]

I want to visit other cities **next time**.
次回はほかの都市を訪れたいです。

1244
next to 〜　　　[〜の隣に]

He works at the coffee shop **next to** the Star Hotel.
彼はスターホテル**の隣の**コーヒーショップで働いています。

---

make *A* from [of] *B* の熟語は受身形で使うことが多いよ。

no more (名詞)

[これ以上の〜はない]

I have **no more** information about it.
それに関する**これ以上の情報は**ありません。

not *A* but *B*

[AではなくB]

He is **not** a doctor **but** a nurse.
彼は医師**ではなく**看護師です。

on foot

[歩いて]

It took about an hour to get there **on foot**.
そこへ行くのに**徒歩で**約1時間かかりました。

on the other hand

[一方では]

Ann likes playing sports. **On the other hand**, her sister likes reading.
アンはスポーツをするのが好きです。**一方**, 彼女の妹は読書が好きです。

on time

[時間どおりに]

The train arrived **on time**.
その列車は**定刻に**到着しました。

on vacation

[休暇で]

I came to Hawaii not **on vacation** but on business.
私は**休暇で**ではなく仕事でハワイに来ました。

once a day [week, month]

[1日[1週間, 1か月]につき1回]

He has to take this medicine **once a day**.
彼は**1日に1回**この薬を服用しなければなりません。

once more

[もう一度]

He wanted to visit France **once more** before he died.
彼は死ぬ前に**もう一度**フランスへ行きたがっていました。

1253
one after another [次々に]

The marathon runners entered the stadium **one after another**.
マラソン走者は**次々に**スタジアムに入ってきました。

1254
one another [お互い]

They looked at **one another** with smiles.
彼らは笑顔で**お互い**を見ました。

1255
One is ~, the other is ... [(2者について)片方は~, 他方は…]

She bought two dresses. **One is** red and **the other is** purple.
彼女はドレスを2着買いました。**1つは**赤で，**もう1つは**紫です。

1256
plan to *do* [~するつもりである]

I'm **planning to take** cooking lessons during summer vacation.
夏休み中に料理講座**を受けるつもりです**。

1257
prepare for ~ [~の準備をする]

We have to **prepare for** the Christmas party.
私たちはクリスマスパーティー**の準備をし**なければなりません。

1258
right away [すぐに]

Certainly, sir. I'll bring it **right away**.
かしこまりました，お客様。**すぐに**お持ちします。

1259
say goodbye [別れを告げる]

Carol left without **saying goodbye**.
キャロルは**別れを告げ**ずに去りました。

1260
say to *oneself* [ひとりごとを言う, 心に思う]

"It will soon be over," he **said to himself**.
「すぐに終わるさ」と彼は**心の中で思い**ました。

あと少し，がんばって！

1261 see A off [A(人)を見送る]

Nancy went to the airport to **see** her friend **off**.
ナンシーは友人**を見送り**に空港に行きました。

1262 show A around ~ [A(人)に〜を案内する]

My aunt **showed** me **around** her town.
おばは私に自分の町**を案内して**くれました。

1263 sleep well [よく眠る]

Did you **sleep well** last night?
昨夜は**よく眠れ**ましたか。

1264 slow down [速度を落とす]

The train **slowed down** and stopped.
列車は**速度を落として**止まりました。

1265 smile at ~ [〜にほほえみかける]

The woman **smiled at** me and asked my name.
その女性は私**にほほえんで**私の名前をたずねました。

1266 so far [今までのところ]

We have won all our games **so far** this season.
今シーズン，私たちは**今までのところ**全勝しています。

1267 so many ~ [非常にたくさんの〜]

There are **so many** questions I want to ask him.
私は彼にたずねたい質問が**とてもたくさん**あります。

1268 some other time [いつか別のときに]

I'm sorry I can't join you tonight. Maybe **some other time**.
今晩はご一緒できなくてごめんね。**またの機会に**，きっとね。

1269
something (形容詞) to *do* ［何か〜すべき…なもの］

I'm thirsty. I want **something** cold **to drink**.
のどが乾いた。**何か**冷たい**飲み物**がほしいな。

1270
sound like 〜 ［〜のように聞こえる］

That **sounds like** a great idea.
すばらしい考え**のように**思います。

1271
speak to 〜 ［〜に話しかける］

I **spoke to** the woman looking at the map.
私は地図を見ている女性**に話しかけました**。

1272
stand for 〜 ［〜を表す，〜の略である］

U.S. **stands for** United States.
U.S. は United States **の略です**。

1273
start with 〜 ［〜で始まる］

The festival **started with** the mayor's speech.
お祭りは市長の演説**で始まりました**。

1274
stay with 〜 ［〜のところに滞在する］

I'm going to **stay with** my uncle in Sydney next weekend.
来週末はシドニーのおじ**のところに滞在する**予定です。

1275
stop by ［立ち寄る］

If you're not busy on Sunday, please **stop by**.
日曜日に忙しくなければ，どうぞ**お立ち寄り**ください。

1276
such as 〜 ［(たとえば)〜のような］

Fruits **such as** peaches and pears are grown in Washington.
ワシントン州ではモモやナシ**のような**果物が栽培されています。

sound＋(形容詞), sound like＋(名詞)で覚えよう。

1277

suffer from ~ [〜に苦しむ]

Many people in the world **suffer from** hunger.
世界では多くの人が飢え**に苦しんで**います。

1278

surf (on) the Internet [インターネットを見て回る]

Fred spends his free time **surfing the Internet.**
フレッドはひまな時間を**インターネットを見て回る**のに費やします。

1279

take a break [休憩する]

Jim always **takes a break** at three in the afternoon.
ジムはいつも午後3時に**休憩をとります**。

1280

take a look at ~ [〜を見る]

David, the DVD player doesn't work. Can you **take a look at** it?
デイビッド，DVDプレーヤーが動かないの。**見て**くれない？

1281

take (a) medicine [薬を飲む]

If you **take** this **medicine**, you will feel better.
この**薬を飲めば**，気分がよくなりますよ。

1282

take a rest [休憩する]

You look tired. Why don't you **take a rest**?
疲れているようですね。**休憩して**はどうですか。

1283

take a seat [席につく，座る]

He told me to **take a seat**.
彼は私に**席に着く**ように言いました。

1284

take a trip [旅行する]

I hear you will **take a trip** to the U.K.
イギリスへ**旅行する**そうですね。

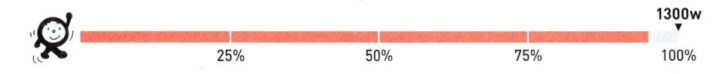

1285
take a walk
[散歩する]

Let's **take a walk** this afternoon.
今日の午後に**散歩**に行きましょう。

1286
take out ~
[~を取り[持ち，連れ]出す]

She **took out** a picture from her bag and showed it to me.
彼女はかばんから1枚の写真**を取り出し**，私に見せてくれました。

1287
tell a lie
[うそをつく]

You mustn't **tell a lie**.
うそをついてはいけません。

1288
(比較級) than any other (単数名詞)
[ほかのどの~よりも…]

Our soccer team is stronger **than any other** team in this city.
私たちのサッカーチームはこの市の**ほかのどの**チーム**よりも**強いです。

1289
thank *A* for ~
[A(人)に~に対する礼を言う]

The man **thanked** me **for** helping him.
その男性は私が助けたこと**に対して礼を言いました**。

1290
these days
[最近]

These days more and more people care about the environment.
最近，ますます多くの人が自然環境を気にかけています。

1291
this is *one's* first time to *do*
[…にとって~することは初めてである]

Is this your first time to come to this town?
この町**に来るのは初めてですか**。

1292
this way
[こちらの方向へ，このようにして]

Come **this way**. I'll show you our office.
どうぞ**こちらへ**。私たちのオフィスをお見せします。

1293
thousands of ~
[何千もの~, たくさんの~]

Thousands of visitors travel to this castle every month.
毎月、何千人もの観光客がこの城を訪れます。

1294
~ times as (形容詞) as A
[Aの~倍…な]

This park is three **times as** large **as** that one.
この公園はあの公園の3倍の広さがあります。

1295
turn ~ over
[~を裏返す]

Ms. Kobayashi, please **turn** the card **over** and look at me.
小林さん、カードを裏返して、私の方を見てください。

1296
used to *do*
[以前はよく~した]

I **used to come** to this park with my grandfather.
私は、以前はよく祖父とこの公園に来ました。

1297
walk around
[歩き回る、散歩する]

At the shopping mall, I just **walked around** and bought nothing.
ショッピングモールでは、ただ歩き回って何も買いませんでした。

1298
would love to *do*
[(ぜひ)~したい]

We **would love to stay** longer, but we have to go.
もっと長くいたいのですが、私たちは行かなければなりません。

1299
write down ~
[~を書きとめる]

I **wrote down** their phone numbers on a piece of paper.
紙に彼らの電話番号を書きとめました。

1300
write to ~
[~に手紙を書く]

Amy **wrote to** her parents every month while she was in Japan.
エイミーは日本にいる間、毎月両親に手紙を書きました。

熟語編が終わった！　いよいよ最後の会話表現編だ。

熟語編　でる度 B

チェックテスト

1 下線の語句の意味を①〜③の中から選びましょう。

(1) **look after** a child
　① 〜の世話をする　② 〜を育てる　③ 〜に従う

(2) go to the park **on foot**
　① ふもとで　　② ついに　　③ 歩いて

(3) **because of** the bad weather
　① 〜を恐れて　② 〜のために　③ 〜の代わりに

(4) I **lay down** for a while.
　① 横になった　② ぐっすり眠った　③ 倒れていた

2 日本語に合うように（　）に適切な語を下の①〜⑥の中から選びましょう。

(1) 私は犬が怖い。　I'm (　　) of dogs.

(2) 彼は花が好きだ。　He is (　　) of flowers.

(3) 私はその町をよく知っている。
　I'm (　　) with the town.

(4) その映画は多くの人に知られている。
　The movie is (　　) to many people.

① interested	② familiar	③ fond
④ afraid	⑤ known	⑥ famous

3 日本語に合うように（　）に英単語を入れましょう。

(1) 10歳のときに　　　　　　　at the (　　　　) of ten

(2) 帰宅するとすぐに　　as soon (　　　　) I get home

(3) 私はまもなく眠りに落ちた。　I fell (　　　　) soon.

(4) 彼は楽しみで歌う。　　　He sings (　　　　) fun.

4 日本語に合うように①～③の中から選びましょう。

(1) 彼の病気が治ったら
when he (① gets　② makes　③ takes) well

(2) すぐに戻る
come back (① soon　② far　③ right) away

(3) 少なくとも10人
at (① last　② least　③ once) ten people

5 (　)に入る語を右の①～⑤の中から選びましょう。

(1) His idea is similar (　　) mine.

(2) This house is made (　　) wood.

(3) She spoke (　　) public.

(4) Look (　　) the word in your dictionary.

(5) I'm satisfied (　　) my grade.

① of
② up
③ with
④ in
⑤ to

正解

1 (1) ① (⇒p.182)　(2) ③ (⇒p.184)　(3) ② (⇒p.171)　(4) ① (⇒p.181)
2 (1) ④ (⇒p.168)　(2) ③ (⇒p.169)　(3) ② (⇒p.169)　(4) ⑤ (⇒p.170)
3 (1) age (⇒p.168)　(2) as (⇒p.167)　(3) asleep (⇒p.173)
(4) for (⇒p.175)
4 (1) ① (⇒p.176)　(2) ③ (⇒p.185)　(3) ② (⇒p.168)
5 (1) ⑤ (⇒p.170)　(2) ① (⇒p.183)　(3) ④ (⇒p.180)　(4) ② (⇒p.182)
(5) ③ (⇒p.170)

過去問にチャレンジ！ ❷

(　　) に入れるのに最も適切なものを 1, 2, 3, 4 の中から一つ選びなさい。

(1) *A:* Where do you (　　) off the bus, Steve?
　　B: At the next stop.
　　1 get　　**2** take　　**3** stand　　**4** make
(2011-1)

(2) Steve didn't get a good score on his math test. He was sick last week, so he couldn't study for it (　　) all.
　　1 at　　**2** for　　**3** on　　**4** by
(2011-2)

(3) *A:* Are you going to Tokyo Disneyland with your family next week?
　　B: Yes. I'm really looking (　　) to it.
　　1 behind　　**2** forward　　**3** still　　**4** along
(2011-2)

(4) In my (　　), high school students should not have part-time jobs. They need to study.
　　1 opinion　　**2** word　　**3** hope　　**4** safety
(2011-2)

正解　(1) **1** (⇒p.147)　(2) **1** (⇒p.154)　(3) **2** (⇒p.153)　(4) **1** (⇒p.151)

日本語訳
(1) A：スティーブ，どこでバスを降りるの？
　　B：次の停留所だよ。
(2) スティーブは数学のテストでよい点数がとれなかった。彼は先週具合が悪かったので，テスト勉強がまったくできなかったのだ。
(3) A：来週，家族と東京ディズニーランドに行くの？
　　B：うん。それをとても楽しみにしているんだ。
(4) 私の意見では，高校生はアルバイトをすべきではない。彼らは勉強する必要がある。

会話表現編

100

会話表現(100) 196

チェックテスト 213

3級によく出る会話表現をまとめました。試験だけでなく，日常英会話でも使える表現ばかりです。

1周目	2周目	3周目
/	/	/

001
Are you all right?
[大丈夫ですか。]

A: You don't look well. **Are you all right?**
B: Yes, I'm just sleepy.
A: 具合が悪そうね。**大丈夫？**
B: うん，眠いだけなんだ。

002
Are you ready to order?
[ご注文は お決まりですか。]

A: **Are you ready to order?**
B: Yes. I'll have a tuna sandwich.
A: **ご注文はお決まりですか。**
B: はい。ツナサンドをお願いします。

003
Can I take a message?
[伝言を承りましょうか。]

A: Hello. Can I speak to Sally, please?
B: I'm sorry, she's out now. **Can I take a message?**
A: もしもし。サリーさんをお願いします。
B: ごめんなさい，今外出しています。**伝言を承りましょうか。**

004
Can you help me with ~?
[~を手伝って もらえますか。]

A: Mark, **can you help me with** cooking?
B: OK, Mom.
A: マーク，料理**を手伝ってくれない？**
B: わかったよ，お母さん。

005
Can you tell me where [when / why / who など] ~?
[どこで[いつ/なぜ/だれが] ~か教えてもらえますか。]

A: Excuse me. **Can you tell me where** the shoe department is?
B: It's on the third floor.
A: すみません。靴売り場は**どこか教えてもらえますか。**
B: 3階にあります。

006
Certainly.
[かしこまりました。]

A: Can I have another cup of coffee, please?
B: **Certainly**, ma'am.
A: コーヒーをもう1杯もらえますか。
B: **かしこまりました**，お客さま。

007 Congratulations! [おめでとう！]

A: I passed the entrance exam.
B: **Congratulations!**
A: 入学試験に受かりました。
B: おめでとう！

008 Do you think so? [そう思いますか。]

A: I think Dan is the best basketball player in our school.
B: **Do you think so?**
A: ダンが学校で一番バスケットボールがじょうずだと思うな。
B: そう思う？

009 Excuse me. [すみませんが。]

A: **Excuse me.** Does this bus go to the city museum?
B: No, take that yellow one.
A: **すみません。** このバスは市立博物館へ行きますか。
B: いいえ，あの黄色いバスに乗ってください。

010 Good job. / You did a great job. [よくできました。]

A: My speech was not very good.
B: I don't think so. **You did a great job.**
A: ぼくのスピーチはいまいちだったよ。
B: そうは思わないわ。**とてもよくできたわよ。**

011 Good luck. [がんばって。]

A: I'm going to play in a game tomorrow.
B: Are you? **Good luck!**
A: 明日，試合に出るんだ。
B: そうなの？ **がんばって！**

012 Guess what? [（会話を切り出すときに）ねえねえ，聞いて］

A: **Guess what?** I'm going to France this summer!
B: That's great. Have fun.
A: **ねえ，聞いて。** 今年の夏にフランスに行くの！
B: それはいいね。楽しんできてね。

会話表現は例文を声に出して覚えよう。

🎧 013〜024

013
Have a good time.
[楽しんできてね。]

A: Mom, I'm going to Frank's house now. I don't need lunch today.
B: All right, Kevin. **Have a good time.**
A: お母さん,今からフランクの家に行ってくる。今日は昼食はいらないよ。
B: わかったわ,ケビン。**楽しんできてね。**

014
Have a nice trip.
[よい旅を。]

A: **Have a nice trip**, Beth. I hope you enjoy yourself in Europe.
B: Thank you. I'll send you a postcard.
A: ベス,**よい旅を。** ヨーロッパで楽しんできてね。
B: ありがとう。絵はがきを送るわね。

015
Help yourself to 〜.
[(食べ物など)をご自由にどうぞ。]

A: **Help yourself to** some more dessert.
B: Thank you.
A: もっとデザート**をご自由に**取って召し上がってください。
B: ありがとう。

016
Here it is.
[(物を差し出して)はい,どうぞ。]

A: Can you pass me the salt?
B: **Here it is.**
A: 塩を取ってくれますか。
B: **はい,どうぞ。**

017
Here you are.
[(物を差し出して)はい,どうぞ。]

A: Do you have a pen?
B: Yes. **Here you are.**
A: ペンを持っていますか。
B: ええ。**はい,どうぞ。**

018
Here's 〜.
[〜をどうぞ。,ここに〜があります。]

A: **Here's** your tea. Do you take sugar or milk?
B: Just a little sugar, please.
A: 紅茶**をどうぞ。** 砂糖やミルクは入れますか。
B: 砂糖を少しだけお願いします。

019 Hold on.
[（電話で）切らないでお待ちください。]

A: May I speak to Mr. Taylor, please?
B: **Hold on** a minute.
A: テイラーさんをお願いします。
B: 少し**お待ちください**。

020 How [What] about 〜?
[〜はどうですか。]

A: Can we go shopping together this weekend?
B: Sure. **How about** Sunday afternoon?
A: 今週末，一緒に買い物に行かない？
B: いいわよ。日曜の午後**はどう**？

021 How about *doing* 〜?
[〜するのはどうですか。]

A: **How about going out** for lunch?
B: Good idea. I'd like to try that new Italian restaurant.
A: ランチを**食べに行かない**？
B: いいわね。あの新しいイタリア料理店に行ってみたいわ。

022 How about you?
[あなたはどうですか。]

A: I'll have some orange juice. **How about you?**
B: Can I have coffee?
A: 私はオレンジジュースを飲むわ。**あなたは？**
B: コーヒーをもらえるかな。

023 How do [did] you like 〜?
[（感想などをたずねて）〜はどうですか[どうでしたか]。]

A: **How did you like** the movie?
B: It was great.
A: 映画**はどうだった**？
B: とてもよかったよ。

024 How is [was] 〜?
[〜はどうですか[どうでしたか]。]

A: **How was** the festival?
B: I had a great time.
A: お祭り**はどうだった**？
B: すごく楽しかったわ。

Here it is. は渡す物に，Here you are. は渡す人に重点を置いた表現だよ。

025 How long does it take to *do* ~?
[～するのにどのくらい時間がかかりますか。]

A: How long does it take to get to the stadium?
B: About fifteen minutes.
A: スタジアムに行くにはどのくらい時間がかかりますか。
B: 15分ほどです。

026 I beg your pardon?
[もう一度おっしゃってください。]

A: My name is John A. Tokarz.
B: I beg your pardon? What is your last name?
A: 私の名前はジョン・A・トカーズです。
B: もう一度おっしゃってください。名字は何ですか。

027 I can't wait.
[待ちきれません。]

A: I hear you're going to a rock concert this weekend.
B: Yes. **I can't wait.**
A: 今週末ロックコンサートに行くんだってね。
B: ええ。待ちきれないわ。

028 I don't think so.
[私はそうは思いません。]

A: Do you think the Giants will win today?
B: No, **I don't think so.**
A: 今日はジャイアンツが勝つと思う?
B: いいや,ぼくはそう思わないな。

029 I hear ~.
[～と聞いています。, ～だそうですね。, ～らしいです。]

A: I hear you're going to join the art club.
B: Yes. I'm interested in painting.
A: 美術部に入るんだってね。
B: そうなの。絵を描くことに興味があるの。

030 I hope ~.
[～と望んでいます。, ～だといいな。]

A: I want to be a pilot in the future.
B: I hope your dreams come true.
A: ぼくは将来パイロットになりたいんだ。
B: 夢がかなうといいわね。

031
I hope so.
[そう望みます。, そうだといいな。]

A: Do you think Kate will come with us?
B: I hope so.
A: ケイトは私たちと一緒に来るかな？
B: **そうだといいけど。**

032
I see.
[なるほど。, わかりました。]

A: Turn left at that corner. You'll find the post office on your right.
B: I see. Thank you.
A: あの角を左に曲がってください。郵便局は右側にあります。
B: **わかりました。** ありがとう。

033
I think so, too.
[私もそう思います。]

A: I think we should clean up the room first.
B: I think so, too.
A: まずは部屋を片づけた方がいいと思うな。
B: **私もそう思うわ。**

034
I'd be glad [happy] to.
[喜んで。]

A: Would you like to come over for some coffee?
B: Sure, **I'd be glad to.**
A: コーヒーを飲みにいらっしゃいませんか。
B: もちろん、**喜んで。**

035
I'd love to.
[ぜひそうしたいです。]

A: We're going to have a party tonight. Why don't you come?
B: I'd love to.
A: 今夜パーティーをします。あなたも来ませんか。
B: **ぜひ行きたいです。**

036
I'll be right back.
[すぐに戻ります。]

A: Excuse me. I think I ordered cheese cake.
B: I'm sorry, sir. **I'll be right back** with it.
A: すみません。チーズケーキを注文したと思うのですが。
B: 申し訳ありません、お客さま。**すぐに持ってまいります。**

I hear や I hope のあとの that は会話では省略するよ。

037
I'll be there.
[そちらへ行きます。]

A: John, I need your help. Can you come here?
B: OK, Mom. **I'll be there** soon.
A: ジョン，手伝ってほしいの。こっちに来られる？
B: わかったよ，お母さん。すぐに**そっちへ行くよ**。

038
I'll think about it.
[考えておきます。]

A: Dad, can I have a watch for my birthday?
B: **I'll think about it.**
A: お父さん，私の誕生日に時計を買ってくれない？
B: **考えておくよ**。

039
I'm afraid (that) ～.
[あいにく [残念ながら] ～です。]

A: Mike, can we go to the beach on Saturday?
B: **I'm afraid** I'm busy this weekend.
A: マイク，土曜日に海に行かない？
B: **あいにく**今週末は忙しいんだ。

040
I'm afraid I can't.
[残念ながら，できません。]

A: Can you help me after lunch?
B: **I'm afraid I can't.** I need to go to the dentist.
A: 昼食後，手伝ってもらえないかな。
B: **悪いけど，できないわ**。歯医者に行かないといけないの。

041
I'm afraid not.
[残念ながら，違います [できません]。]

A: Is there a bathroom on this floor?
B: No, **I'm afraid not.** But there is one on the third floor.
A: この階にトイレはありますか。
B: いえ，**申し訳ありませんが，ありません**。3階にあります。

042
I'm coming.
[今行きます。]

A: Steve, dinner is ready.
B: OK. **I'm coming.**
A: スティーブ，夕食ができたわよ。
B: わかった。**今行くよ**。

043 I'm full. [お腹がいっぱいです。]

A: Would you like some more salad?
B: No, thank you. **I'm full.**
A: サラダをもっといかがですか。
B: いえ、けっこうです。**お腹がいっぱいです。**

044 I'm glad you like it. [気に入ってくれてうれしいです。]

A: Thank you very much for such a lovely present.
B: **I'm glad you like it.**
A: こんなすばらしい贈り物をどうもありがとう。
B: **気に入ってくれてうれしいよ。**

045 I'm just looking. [(店で)見ているだけです。]

A: May I help you?
B: **I'm just looking**, thank you.
A: 何かお探しですか。
B: **ただ見ているだけです**、ありがとう。

046 I'm not from here. [ここの者ではありません。]

A: Excuse me. Is there a bank around here?
B: Sorry, but **I'm not from here.**
A: すみません。この辺りに銀行はありますか。
B: ごめんなさい、**ここの者ではないのです。**

047 I'm not sure. [よくわかりません。]

A: Are you going fishing tomorrow?
B: **I'm not sure.** It depends on the weather.
A: 明日は釣りに行くの?
B: **わからないな。** 天気次第だね。

048 I'm sure 〜. [きっと〜だと思います。]

A: **I'm sure** you will pass the exam.
B: I hope so.
A: 君は**きっと**試験に合格する**と思う**よ。
B: そうだといいわ。

そろそろ終わりが見えてきたよ。

049 Is anything wrong? [何か問題がありますか。]

A: You're not eating the pizza. **Is anything wrong?**
B: Well, I don't like seafood very much.
A: ピザを食べていないじゃない。何か問題があるの？
B: いやあ，シーフードはあまり好きじゃないんだ。

050 It looks like rain. [雨が降りそうです。]

A: It looks like rain.
B: Don't forget to take an umbrella with you.
A: 雨が降りそうだよ。
B: 傘を持っていくのを忘れないでね。

051 It's my pleasure. [どういたしまして。]

A: Thank you for the delicious dinner.
B: It's my pleasure.
A: おいしいディナーをありがとうございました。
B: どういたしまして。

052 It's time for 〜. [〜の時間です。]

A: Kevin, **it's time for** bed.
B: All right, Mom.
A: ケビン，寝る時間よ。
B: わかったよ，お母さん。

053 It's time to *do* 〜. [〜する時間です。]

A: Pat, **it's time to** get up.
B: I want to sleep more.
A: パット，起きる時間よ。
B: もっと寝ていたいよ。

054 Just a moment [minute]. [ちょっとお待ちください。]

A: Hello. I'm here to see Mr. White. My name is Allen.
B: Just a moment, please.
A: こんにちは。ホワイトさんに会いに来ました。私の名前はアレンです。
B: ちょっとお待ちください。

055
Let me see.
[（考えながら）ええと。]

A: How many people are coming to the party?
B: **Let me see.** Jeff can't come, so six people.
A: パーティーには何人来るの？
B: **ええと。** ジェフが来られないから，6人だね。

056
May [Can] I help you?
[いらっしゃいませ。何かお探しですか。]

A: Good morning, **may I help you?**
B: Yes, I'm looking for a nice present for my mother.
A: おはようございます。**何かお探しですか。**
B: はい，母にすてきなプレゼントを探しています。

057
Me, too.
[私も。]

A: I want to go skiing this winter.
B: **Me, too.**
A: 今年の冬はスキーに行きたいな。
B: **私もよ。**

058
Nice talking to you.
[お話ができてよかったです。]

A: Well, I have to leave now. **Nice talking to you.**
B: Thank you for coming today.
A: もう行かなければ。**お話ができてよかったです。**
B: 今日は来てくださってありがとう。

059
Nice to see you again.
[また会えてうれしいです。]

A: **Nice to see you again**, Lisa.
B: **Nice to see you again** too, Brian.
A: **また会えてうれしいよ**，リサ。
B: 私も**また会えてうれしいわ**，ブライアン。

060
No, not really.
[いや，それほどでもないです。]

A: Is the new French restaurant very expensive?
B: **No, not really.**
A: その新しいフランス料理店はとても高いの？
B: **いや，それほどでもないよ。**

Nice talking to you. は別れるときに言うよ。

061
No, not yet.
[いいえ，まだです。]

A: Have you finished lunch?
B: No, not yet.
A: 昼食は済ませましたか。
B: いいえ，まだです。

062
No problem.
[いいですよ，どういたしまして。]

A: Could you drive me to the station, Dad?
B: No problem.
A: お父さん，車で駅まで送ってもらえない？
B: いいよ。

063
No, thanks [thank you].
[いいえ，けっこうです。]

A: Would you like something to drink?
B: No, thanks.
A: 飲み物はいかが？
B: いいえ，けっこうです。

064
Of course.
[もちろん。いいですよ。]

A: Excuse me. Can we order?
B: Of course.
A: すみません。注文してもいいですか。
B: もちろんです。

065
Of course not.
[もちろん違います。]

A: Are you going to give up your dream?
B: Of course not.
A: 夢をあきらめるつもりなの？
B: もちろんそんなことはないよ。

066
(Please) take your time.
[（急がないので）ゆっくりしてください。]

A: I'm sorry, I'm going to be a little late.
B: That's OK. **Take your time.**
A: ごめん。少し遅れるんだ。
B: 大丈夫よ。ゆっくりして。

067 Same to you.
[あなたもね。]

A: Have a nice weekend.
B: **Same to you.**
A: いい週末を。
B: 君もね。

068 See you later.
[またあとでね。]

A: Well, I'm in a hurry. **See you later.**
B: OK. Bye.
A: ええと，急いでいるの。またね。
B: わかった。じゃあね。

069 So do [am] I.
[私も。]

A: Tony really likes baseball.
B: **So do I.**
A: トニーは本当に野球が好きね。
B: ぼくもだよ。

070 Something is wrong with ～.
[～の調子がどこかおかしい。]

A: Dad, **something is wrong with** this computer.
B: Let me take a look at it.
A: お父さん，このコンピューターの調子がどこかおかしいの。
B: ちょっと見せてごらん。

071 Sounds good [nice, great].
[よさそうですね。]

A: How about going to the movies tonight?
B: **Sounds good.**
A: 今夜，映画を見に行かない？
B: いいね。

072 Sure.
[もちろん。いいですよ。]

A: Can I use the bathroom?
B: **Sure.**
A: トイレをお借りしてもいいですか。
B: いいですよ。

もうすぐ終わりだ。あと一息！

🎧 073 ~ 084

073 Take care.
[（別れのあいさつとして）じゃあね。，気をつけてね。]

A: Oh, it's time to go home. See you tomorrow.
B: Take care.
A: あら，帰る時間だわ。また明日ね。
B: じゃあね。

074 Thanks anyway.
[とにかくありがとう。]

A: Sorry, but I'm a stranger here.
B: That's fine. **Thanks anyway.**
A: ごめんなさい，この辺りのことはよく知らないんです。
B: いいんですよ。とにかくありがとう。

075 Thanks [Thank you] for *doing* ~.
[～してくれてありがとう。]

A: Thanks for inviting me to the party.
B: Not at all. I'm glad you came.
A: パーティーに**招待してくれてありがとう**。
B: どういたしまして。来てくれてうれしいよ。

076 (That) sounds like fun.
[楽しそうですね。]

A: I'm going to a baseball game. Do you want to come, too?
B: Sounds like fun.
A: 野球の試合を見に行くんだ。君も来ない？
B: **楽しそうね。**

077 That would be great [nice].
[それはいいですね。]

A: I'm baking a cake now. Would you like to come over?
B: That would be great.
A: 今，ケーキを焼いているの。こっちに来ない？
B: **それはいいね。**

078 That's a good idea.
[それはいい考えです。]

A: Shall we get something nice for Lisa's birthday?
B: That's a good idea.
A: リサの誕生日に何かすてきなものを買おうか。
B: **それはいい考えね。**

079 That's all. [それで全部です。]

A: Anything else?
B: **That's all**, thanks.
A: ほかに何か必要ですか。
B: **それで全部です**，ありがとう。

080 That's fine (with ~). [(~にとって)それで大丈夫です。]

A: Can we have a meeting on Friday afternoon?
B: **That's fine with** me.
A: 金曜日の午後にミーティングができますか。
B: 私は**大丈夫ですよ**。

081 That's right. [そのとおりです。]

A: You're on the basketball team, aren't you?
B: **That's right**.
A: あなたはバスケットボール部に入っているんですよね?
B: そうですよ。

082 That's too bad. [それは気の毒[残念]です。]

A: I couldn't go camping because I had a cold.
B: **That's too bad**.
A: 風邪をひいていたので，キャンプに行けなかったんだ。
B: **それはお気の毒に**。

083 That's very kind of you. [ご親切にありがとう。]

A: You can use my car if you like.
B: **That's very kind of you**.
A: よかったら私の車を使っていいですよ。
B: **それはご親切にありがとう**。

084 This is ~. [(電話で)こちらは~です。]

A: Hello. **This is** Nick. Is Linda there?
B: Hold on, please.
A: もしもし。**こちらはニックです**。リンダはいますか。
B: お待ちください。

Thank you for *doing* は並べ換え問題でもよく出るよ。

🎧 085～096

085 What do you do? [（職業は）何をしていますか。]

A: Hi, I'm Helen. You're Tom's friend, aren't you? **What do you do?**
B: Hi, Helen. I'm a teacher.
A: こんにちは、ヘレンです。トムのお友だちですよね？ **お仕事は何ですか。**
B: やあ、ヘレン。ぼくは教師をしています。

086 What do you think of ～? [～をどう思いますか。]

A: What do you think of this town?
B: I like it, but it's too cold in winter.
A: この町**をどう思いますか。**
B: 好きですが、冬が寒すぎます。

087 What happened? [何があったのですか。]

A: Paula, **what happened?**
B: I fell off my bike.
A: ポーラ、**何があったの？**
B: 自転車で転んだの。

088 What would you like (for ～)? [（～には）何がほしいですか。]

A: What would you like for dinner?
B: How about beef stew?
A: 夕食**は何がいい？**
B: ビーフシチューはどうかな。

089 What's the matter with ～? [～はどうしたのですか。]

A: What's the matter with you?
B: I've had a headache since this morning.
A: **どうしたのですか。**
B: 今朝から頭が痛いのです。

090 What's the problem? [どうしたのですか。]

A: You don't look well. **What's the problem?**
B: I didn't do well on my math test.
A: 元気がないわね。**どうしたの？**
B: 数学のテストの出来が悪かったんだ。

210

091 What's up?

[どうしたの？
(あいさつとして)元気？]

A: John, can we talk now?
B: Sure. **What's up?**
A: ジョン，ちょっといい？
B: いいよ。**どうしたの？**

092 What's wrong with ～?

[～はどうしたのですか。]

A: **What's wrong with** Bill? He's been absent for three days.
B: I hear he broke his leg.
A: ビル**はどうしたのかな**。3日間休んでいるね。
B: 脚を骨折したらしいわ。

093 Why don't we ～?

[(一緒に)～しませんか。]

A: **Why don't we** go for a walk after lunch?
B: Sounds nice.
A: 昼食後に散歩に行き**ませんか**。
B: いいわね。

094 Why don't you ～?

[～してはどうですか。]

A: I'm going to Sydney, but I don't know where to stay.
B: **Why don't you** ask Ben? He used to live there.
A: シドニーに行くんだけど，どこに滞在すればいいかわからないんだ。
B: ベンに聞いた**らどう？** 彼は以前そこに住んでいたわよ。

095 Why not?

[(否定文を受けて)なぜですか。,
(提案などを受けて)もちろんです。]

A: I want to go with you, but I can't.
B: **Why not?**
A: あなたと一緒に行きたいんだけど，だめなの。
B: **どうして？**

096 Would you like to *do* ～?

[～しませんか。,
～したいですか。]

A: **Would you like to go** hiking on Sunday?
B: I'd love to.
A: 日曜日にハイキングに**行かない？**
B: ええ，ぜひ。

097
Yes, speaking. [(電話で) はい，私です。]

A: Hello. May I speak to Liz, please?
B: **Yes, speaking.**
A: もしもし。リズさんをお願いします。
B: はい，私です。

098
You can do it. [あなたならできますよ。]

A: I have too much homework. I can't do it all today.
B: Take it easy. **You can do it.**
A: 宿題がたくさんありすぎる。今日全部できないよ。
B: 落ち着いて。**あなたならできるわ。**

099
(You) go ahead. [(お先に) どうぞ。]

A: Tina, let's go to the cafeteria.
B: I have to go to the library first. **Go ahead**, and I'll come later.
A: ティナ，カフェテリアに行こうよ。
B: その前に図書室に行かなくちゃ。**先に行ってて。**あとで合流するから。

100
You're welcome. [どういたしまして。]

A: Thank you for your help.
B: **You're welcome.**
A: 手伝ってくれてありがとう。
B: どういたしまして。

会話表現編

チェックテスト

1 日本語に合うように①〜③の中から選びましょう。

(1) ゆっくりしてください。
Take your (① home ② age ③ time).

(2) がんばって。
Good (① work ② job ③ luck).

(3) どういたしまして。
It's my (① welcome ② pleasure ③ hope).

2 次の質問に合う応答を下の①〜⑥の中から選びましょう。

(1) Do you have a pen?　　　　　　　(　　)

(2) Why don't you come to the party?　(　　)

(3) Have you finished your homework?　(　　)

(4) Anything else?　　　　　　　　　(　　)

(5) Can I speak to Jane, please?　　　(　　)

(6) May I help you?　　　　　　　　(　　)

> ① No, not yet.　② Here you are.
> ③ Yes, speaking.　④ No, I'm just looking.
> ⑤ I'd love to.　⑥ That's all.

ついにやったね！　ここまでできたら合格まちがいなし！

3 日本語に合うように（　）の語を並べかえ記号を書きましょう。

(1) 来てくれてありがとう。
Thank (① for ② coming ③ you).　　（　）（　）（　）

(2) ご親切にありがとう。
That's very (① you ② of ③ kind).　　（　）（　）（　）

(3) 気に入ってくれてうれしいです。
I'm (① like ② glad ③ you) it.　　（　）（　）（　）

(4) 散歩に行くのはどうですか。
How (① a walk ② about ③ for ④ going)?
　　　　　　　　　　　　　　　　　（　）（　）（　）（　）

4 対話が成り立つように，〈　〉には適する疑問詞を書き，（　）には適する語を右の①～⑤の中から選びましょう。

(1) A: 〈　　　　　〉 was my report?
　　B: I'm (　　　) I haven't read it yet.

(2) A: Would you (　　　) to go shopping?
　　B: 〈　　　　　〉 not?

(3) A: 〈　　　　　〉 is the problem?
　　B: Something is (　　　) with my camera.

① sure
② wrong
③ like
④ hope
⑤ afraid

正解

1 (1) ③ (⇒p.206)　　(2) ③ (⇒p.197)　　(3) ② (⇒p.204)
2 (1) ② (⇒p.198)　　(2) ⑤ (⇒p.201)　　(3) ① (⇒p.206)　　(4) ⑥ (⇒p.209)
　　(5) ③ (⇒p.212)　　(6) ④ (⇒p.203)
3 (1) ③①② (⇒p.208)　　(2) ③②① (⇒p.209)　　(3) ②③① (⇒p.203)
　　(4) ②④③① (⇒p.199)
4 (1) How (⇒p.199) ／⑤ (⇒p.202)　　(2) ③ (⇒p.211) ／Why (⇒p.211)
　　(3) What (⇒p.210) ／② (⇒p.207)

さくいん

単語編

A

- above 133
- abroad 88
- absent 84
- accident 64
- across 47
- act 96
- action 111
- activity 103
- actor 34
- actress 70
- actually 131
- add 96
- address 103
- adult 103
- adventure 70
- advice 111
- afraid 40
- again 43
- against 89
- age 103
- ago 44
- agree 54
- ahead 88
- air 61
- airport 61
- alarm 70
- alive 128
- all 48
- almost 87
- alone 87
- along 89
- aloud 131
- already 45
- also 43
- although 132
- a.m. 20
- among 132
- angry 41
- animal 19
- another 41
- answer 52
- anymore 87
- anyone 48
- anything 90
- anytime 130
- anyway 131
- anywhere 131
- apartment 103
- appear 96
- aquarium 103
- area 24
- arm 103
- around 43
- arrest 96
- arrive 17
- asleep 124
- athlete 64
- attack 56
- attend 94
- aunt 24
- award 111

B

- badly 131
- bake 18
- bakery 64
- band 22
- bank 64
- barbecue 70
- basket 104
- bathroom 70
- battle 104
- beach 34
- beautiful 39
- because 46
- become 13
- before 43
- begin 16
- beginner 70
- beginning 111
- behind 90
- believe 52
- beside 89
- best 37
- better 38
- between 47
- bicycle 64
- bike 61
- billion 111
- blackboard 111
- block 104
- body 104
- boil 96
- bookstore 32
- boring 84
- borrow 16
- both 90

215

☐ bottle	79	☐ centimeter	104	☐ comfortable	124
☐ bottom	71	☐ central	124	☐ comic	112
☐ break	17	☐ century	65	☐ common	124
☐ bridge	71	☐ ceremony	105	☐ communicate	97
☐ bright	124	☐ chance	61	☐ communication	112
☐ bring	12	☐ change	17	☐ company	24
☐ broken	84	☐ cheap	84	☐ computer	71
☐ build	14	☐ cheaply	89	☐ concert	27
☐ building	30	☐ check	54	☐ contact	54
☐ burn	96	☐ cheer	97	☐ contest	20
☐ business	104	☐ cheerful	128	☐ continent	71
☐ busy	38	☐ chef	105	☐ continue	56
☐ button	104	☐ child	65	☐ control	97
☐ by	47	☐ chimpanzee	23	☐ convenience	34
		☐ Chinese	65	☐ cookie	24
C		☐ chocolate	26	☐ corner	105
☐ cafeteria	61	☐ choose	17	☐ cost	52
☐ call	10	☐ circle	61	☐ costume	105
☐ camera	32	☐ classmate	79	☐ could	48
☐ camp	112	☐ classroom	79	☐ country	23
☐ cancel	94	☐ clean	14	☐ course	71
☐ capital	112	☐ clever	124	☐ court	71
☐ captain	65	☐ climate	112	☐ cousin	27
☐ care	26	☐ climb	94	☐ cover	16
☐ careful	124	☐ close	39	☐ cross	52
☐ carefully	132	☐ closet	105	☐ crowded	81
☐ carry	56	☐ cloth	65	☐ cry	57
☐ castle	112	☐ clothes	32	☐ culture	34
☐ catch	54	☐ cloudy	84	☐ custom	105
☐ cause	97	☐ coach	71	☐ customer	61
☐ ceiling	104	☐ coat	66	☐ cut	94
☐ celebrate	54	☐ collect	52	☐ cute	125
☐ celebration	65	☐ college	30		
☐ cell phone	65	☐ color	34	**D**	
☐ center	65	☐ comedy	71	☐ daily	81

☐ damage	112	☐ discover	97	☐ environment	73
☐ danger	112	☐ dish	32	☐ escape	98
☐ dangerous	84	☐ doctor	21	☐ especially	88
☐ dark	125	☐ doghouse	27	☐ even	46
☐ date	19	☐ dollar	66	☐ event	32
☐ daughter	30	☐ doughnut	72	☐ ever	45
☐ dear	37	☐ draw	18	☐ everywhere	46
☐ death	113	☐ dream	61	☐ exam	62
☐ decide	12	☐ dress	66	☐ examination	113
☐ decorate	97	☐ drive	14	☐ example	66
☐ decoration	72	☐ drugstore	106	☐ excellent	125
☐ deep	84	☐ during	47	☐ exchange	57
☐ delicious	41			☐ excited	81
☐ deliver	52	**E**		☐ exciting	41
☐ dentist	72	☐ each	40	☐ expect	55
☐ department store		☐ ear	62	☐ expensive	82
	105	☐ early	45	☐ experience	66
☐ description	72	☐ earthquake	113	☐ explain	98
☐ desert	113	☐ easily	87	☐ express	98
☐ design	94	☐ easy	82	☐ expression	114
☐ dessert	72	☐ either	87		
☐ destroy	57	☐ elderly	128	**F**	
☐ dictionary	21	☐ elementary	85	☐ fact	73
☐ die	52	☐ elephant	19	☐ factory	26
☐ difference	105	☐ elevator	113	☐ fail	98
☐ different	39	☐ else	87	☐ fair	30
☐ difficult	40	☐ e-mail	23	☐ fall	53
☐ difficulty	113	☐ end	32	☐ familiar	85
☐ digital	125	☐ enemy	113	☐ famous	37
☐ dining	72	☐ energy	113	☐ far	46
☐ direct	97	☐ enjoy	11	☐ farm	32
☐ director	106	☐ enjoyable	85	☐ farmer	25
☐ dirty	128	☐ enough	39	☐ fast	82
☐ disappear	97	☐ enter	53	☐ favorite	38
☐ discount	72	☐ entrance	72	☐ feed	98

☐ feel	17	
☐ female	81	
☐ fence	66	
☐ festival	19	
☐ fever	106	
☐ few	82	
☐ field	106	
☐ fight	53	
☐ figure	106	
☐ finally	87	
☐ find	11	
☐ fine	40	
☐ finish	11	
☐ fire	62	
☐ firework	114	
☐ first	43	
☐ fit	57	
☐ fix	98	
☐ flag	114	
☐ flight	106	
☐ floor	29	
☐ fly	55	
☐ fold	98	
☐ follow	55	
☐ food	21	
☐ foreign	41	
☐ forest	32	
☐ forget	55	
☐ fork	114	
☐ free	37	
☐ freedom	114	
☐ French	30	
☐ fresh	85	
☐ fridge	114	
☐ friendly	125	
☐ friendship	114	
☐ fruit	73	
☐ full	83	
☐ fun	22	
☐ funny	85	
☐ furniture	106	
☐ future	30	

G

☐ garbage	106
☐ garden	25
☐ gate	73
☐ generation	114
☐ German	66
☐ gesture	115
☐ gift	73
☐ give	11
☐ glad	40
☐ glass	115
☐ glove	115
☐ goal	73
☐ god	34
☐ goldfish	73
☐ government	30
☐ grade	66
☐ graduate	17
☐ gram	115
☐ grandfather	67
☐ grandmother	33
☐ grandparent	115
☐ grandson	107
☐ grass	107
☐ greet	98
☐ greeting	115
☐ group	28

☐ grow	11
☐ guess	57
☐ guide	107
☐ gym	35

H

☐ half	83
☐ hallway	107
☐ hamburger	67
☐ hang	94
☐ happen	14
☐ hard	44
☐ headache	73
☐ health	74
☐ healthy	125
☐ heat	115
☐ heavy	83
☐ height	60
☐ helpful	128
☐ hero	107
☐ herself	90
☐ hide	99
☐ hike	99
☐ hill	74
☐ hint	115
☐ history	28
☐ hit	55
☐ hobby	74
☐ hold	13
☐ hole	116
☐ holiday	107
☐ homesick	83
☐ homestay	74
☐ hometown	67
☐ hope	12

☐ horizon	107
☐ horse	116
☐ hospital	30
☐ host	116
☐ hour	23
☐ huge	128
☐ human	85
☐ hungry	42
☐ hunt	99
☐ hurricane	60
☐ hurry	55
☐ hurt	53
☐ husband	35

I

☐ ice	26
☐ ice cream	60
☐ idea	25
☐ if	46
☐ illness	107
☐ imagine	57
☐ importance	116
☐ important	41
☐ impossible	128
☐ impress	99
☐ information	21
☐ injure	99
☐ ink	116
☐ inside	88
☐ instead	131
☐ instrument	31
☐ interesting	42
☐ international	128
☐ Internet	67
☐ interview	99

☐ introduce	57
☐ invent	55
☐ invite	12
☐ island	33
☐ Italian	40

J

☐ jazz	31
☐ jeans	74
☐ job	21
☐ jog	53
☐ join	13
☐ judge	99
☐ juice	116
☐ jump	57
☐ junior	81
☐ just	44

K

☐ keep	14
☐ key	74
☐ kid	74
☐ kill	55
☐ kilogram	74
☐ kind	21
☐ kitchen	75
☐ kitten	21
☐ knock	94

L

☐ land	75
☐ language	75
☐ last	10
☐ late	39
☐ later	44

☐ latest	125
☐ laugh	99
☐ law	75
☐ lay	100
☐ lead	100
☐ leaf	116
☐ learn	11
☐ leave	17
☐ lend	17
☐ less	85
☐ lesson	25
☐ let	95
☐ letter	28
☐ librarian	75
☐ library	23
☐ license	116
☐ life	29
☐ line	67
☐ list	108
☐ little	38
☐ living room	67
☐ local	125
☐ locker	67
☐ lonely	129
☐ look	10
☐ lose	53
☐ lost	42
☐ loud	81
☐ low	129
☐ luckily	89
☐ lucky	129

M

☐ machine	35
☐ magazine	33

☐ main	42	☐ musician	28	☐ once	46
☐ make	10	☐ must	48	☐ one	48
☐ male	82			☐ online	131
☐ manager	67	**N**		☐ opinion	109
☐ mark	75	☐ narrow	85	☐ order	58
☐ marry	100	☐ national	81	☐ other	37
☐ maybe	87	☐ native	42	☐ outdoor	129
☐ mayor	75	☐ natural	126	☐ outside	45
☐ meal	68	☐ nature	33	☐ oven	109
☐ mean	58	☐ necessary	126	☐ over	47
☐ meat	75	☐ necklace	76	☐ overseas	132
☐ medal	76	☐ need	11	☐ oversleep	95
☐ medicine	25	☐ neighbor	117	☐ own	83
☐ meeting	24	☐ neighborhood	108	☐ owner	117
☐ member	33	☐ nephew	117		
☐ memory	108	☐ nervous	43	**P**	
☐ message	33	☐ never	44	☐ page	62
☐ meter	80	☐ newspaper	24	☐ pain	118
☐ middle	108	☐ next	43	☐ paint	15
☐ midnight	108	☐ noise	117	☐ painting	76
☐ mild	129	☐ noisy	129	☐ pajamas	109
☐ million	62	☐ noon	108	☐ pancake	76
☐ minute	28	☐ note	117	☐ panda	62
☐ mirror	117	☐ nothing	90	☐ paper	35
☐ miss	16	☐ notice	28	☐ parade	60
☐ mix	100	☐ novel	117	☐ parent	22
☐ model	108	☐ nurse	76	☐ part	22
☐ money	20			☐ part-time	45
☐ month	25	**O**		☐ pass	56
☐ most	39	☐ offer	100	☐ passenger	118
☐ mountain	62	☐ office	29	☐ pay	53
☐ move	12	☐ official	129	☐ peace	118
☐ movie	20	☐ often	44	☐ peaceful	129
☐ museum	68	☐ oil	117	☐ perfect	86
☐ musical	108	☐ Olympic	60	☐ perform	56

☐ performance	118	
☐ person	31	
☐ phone	62	
☐ photo	63	
☐ pick	18	
☐ pie	31	
☐ pizza	26	
☐ place	22	
☐ plan	23	
☐ plane	35	
☐ planet	109	
☐ plant	13	
☐ pleasure	109	
☐ p.m.	19	
☐ pocket	109	
☐ point	68	
☐ police	109	
☐ polite	130	
☐ pollution	68	
☐ pool	29	
☐ poor	86	
☐ popular	38	
☐ port	118	
☐ possible	82	
☐ postcard	118	
☐ poster	63	
☐ powerful	130	
☐ practice	23	
☐ prepare	95	
☐ present	63	
☐ president	35	
☐ pretty	88	
☐ price	76	
☐ prize	27	
☐ problem	63	

☐ produce	100
☐ professional	41
☐ program	118
☐ project	76
☐ promise	76
☐ protect	53
☐ public	86
☐ pull	100
☐ pumpkin	25
☐ puppy	109
☐ push	58
☐ put	13

Q

☐ queen	77
☐ question	35
☐ quiet	126

R

☐ race	63
☐ radio	110
☐ rain	13
☐ raise	95
☐ reach	54
☐ ready	39
☐ realize	100
☐ reason	68
☐ receive	18
☐ recipe	68
☐ record	101
☐ recycle	101
☐ relax	58
☐ remember	15
☐ repeat	95
☐ report	27

☐ resort	118
☐ rest	77
☐ restaurant	20
☐ return	15
☐ ride	54
☐ right	38
☐ rise	95
☐ road	33
☐ rock	77
☐ rocket	119
☐ round	126
☐ rule	63

S

☐ sad	82
☐ sadness	119
☐ safely	131
☐ safety	119
☐ sail	58
☐ salad	35
☐ sale	68
☐ salesclerk	119
☐ same	40
☐ sandwich	68
☐ save	15
☐ say	15
☐ scared	126
☐ scarf	63
☐ scene	119
☐ schedule	110
☐ schoolwork	77
☐ science	69
☐ science fiction	77
☐ scientist	24
☐ scissors	119

Word	Page	Word	Page	Word	Page
☐ score	110	☐ sincerely	88	☐ stadium	120
☐ secret	69	☐ sir	78	☐ stair	121
☐ section	77	☐ skate	18	☐ stamp	60
☐ see	10	☐ skill	120	☐ star	63
☐ seem	95	☐ sleep	15	☐ state	121
☐ sell	16	☐ slice	69	☐ station	26
☐ send	12	☐ smart	86	☐ statue	121
☐ sentence	77	☐ smell	56	☐ steak	121
☐ serious	130	☐ smile	95	☐ steal	59
☐ serve	58	☐ smoke	101	☐ stew	78
☐ several	126	☐ snack	78	☐ still	45
☐ shake	58	☐ sneaker	120	☐ stomach	121
☐ shampoo	119	☐ snow	16	☐ stop	24
☐ shape	119	☐ snowboard	59	☐ store	20
☐ share	54	☐ snowy	126	☐ storm	110
☐ shine	101	☐ sofa	110	☐ straight	89
☐ shock	101	☐ softly	132	☐ stranger	121
☐ shoot	101	☐ soldier	120	☐ street	27
☐ short	86	☐ solve	101	☐ strong	127
☐ should	48	☐ someday	89	☐ subject	19
☐ shout	58	☐ someone	90	☐ such	82
☐ show	13	☐ something	90	☐ suddenly	89
☐ shower	120	☐ sometimes	88	☐ sugar	121
☐ shrine	120	☐ son	23	☐ suit	121
☐ shut	56	☐ sorry	38	☐ suitcase	122
☐ shuttle	110	☐ sound	14	☐ sunny	86
☐ shy	83	☐ southern	127	☐ sunrise	122
☐ sick	38	☐ space	25	☐ sunset	122
☐ side	69	☐ Spanish	31	☐ supermarket	34
☐ sight	110	☐ speak	14	☐ support	102
☐ sightseeing	120	☐ special	37	☐ sure	39
☐ sign	77	☐ speech	33	☐ surprised	40
☐ silent	83	☐ speed	120	☐ surprising	130
☐ simple	126	☐ spell	101	☐ survive	102
☐ since	47	☐ spend	18	☐ sweater	78

☐ sweet	127
☐ symbol	122
☐ system	78

T

☐ take	10
☐ taste	56
☐ tasty	130
☐ telephone	78
☐ tell	11
☐ temperature	122
☐ textbook	69
☐ than	46
☐ theater	64
☐ thick	127
☐ thing	28
☐ thirsty	127
☐ thousand	78
☐ throw	59
☐ ticket	28
☐ tie	110
☐ tiger	29
☐ tight	130
☐ tired	42
☐ together	44
☐ tonight	45
☐ tool	69
☐ top	69
☐ touch	96
☐ tour	69
☐ tourist	70
☐ tournament	36
☐ toward	132
☐ toy	20
☐ tradition	122
☐ traditional	127
☐ train	34
☐ travel	12
☐ trick	78
☐ trip	21
☐ trouble	111
☐ true	83
☐ try	12
☐ turn	18
☐ twice	88
☐ twin	122
☐ type	79
☐ typhoon	122

U

☐ uncle	29
☐ understand	16
☐ unfortunately	132
☐ uniform	64
☐ university	22
☐ until	47
☐ upset	127
☐ upstairs	132
☐ useful	42
☐ usual	86
☐ usually	45

V

☐ vacation	22
☐ vegetable	31
☐ video	80
☐ view	79
☐ village	79
☐ visitor	27
☐ voice	111
☐ volunteer	22

W

☐ wait	16
☐ waiter	79
☐ wake	59
☐ wallet	79
☐ war	36
☐ warm	42
☐ waste	102
☐ watch	15
☐ way	27
☐ wear	14
☐ weather	26
☐ website	29
☐ wedding	64
☐ weekend	20
☐ welcome	59
☐ well	37
☐ wet	130
☐ when	46
☐ while	47
☐ whole	127
☐ wide	86
☐ wife	31
☐ wild	41
☐ win	13
☐ wine	123
☐ wing	123
☐ winner	29
☐ wish	102
☐ without	90
☐ wonder	96
☐ wonderful	84
☐ wood	70

□ word	26
□ work	10
□ worker	60
□ worry	15
□ writer	31

□ wrong	43

Y

□ yet	44

Z

□ zoo	19

熟語編

A

□ a couple of ~	166
□ a few ~	138
□ a friend of mine	166
□ a glass of ~	138
□ a little too (形容詞)	138
□ a lot	138
□ a lot of ~	138
□ a number of ~	166
□ a pair of ~	138
□ (a) part of ~	166
□ a piece of ~	138
□ a sheet of ~	138
□ a slice of ~	139
□ after a while	139
□ after school	139
□ agree with ~	139
□ all day (long)	166
□ all night (long)	166
□ all over the world	139
□ all the time	166
□ all the way	166
□ ~ and so on	167
□ another (形容詞) minute(s)	167
□ anything else	139
□ arrive in [at, on] ~	139

□ as (副詞 / 形容詞) as A can	139
□ as many (名詞) as ~	167
□ as much as A can	167
□ as much as possible	167
□ as soon as ~	167
□ as usual	140
□ A as well as B	167
□ as you know	167
□ ask (A) for ~	140
□ ask A to do	140
□ at a time	168
□ at first	140
□ at last	140
□ at least	168
□ at once	168
□ at school	140
□ at the age of ~	168
□ at the end of ~	140
□ at the foot of ~	168

B

□ be able to do	140
□ be absent from ~	141
□ be afraid of ~	168
□ be at home	168
□ be at one's desk	168
□ be back	169
□ be born	141

☐ be busy with ~	169	☐ become friends with ~	143
☐ be careful (about ~)	169	☐ belong to ~	171
☐ be close to ~	169	☐ between *A* and *B*	143
☐ be covered with ~	141	☐ both *A* and *B*	143
☐ be different from ~	141	☐ both of ~	143
☐ be familiar with ~	169	☐ brush *one's* teeth	171
☐ be famous for ~	141	☐ by *oneself*	143
☐ be filled with ~	169	☐ by the way	171
☐ be fond of ~	169		
☐ be full of ~	141	**C**	
☐ be glad to *do*	141	☐ call *A* back	171
☐ be good at ~	141	☐ care about ~	172
☐ be in a hurry	142	☐ catch a cold	172
☐ be in trouble	142	☐ change trains	172
☐ be interested in ~	142	☐ cheer up ~	172
☐ be known as ~	169	☐ clean up ~	143
☐ be known to ~	170	☐ come back	144
☐ be late for ~	142	☐ come home	144
☐ be out	142	☐ come true	144
☐ be over	170	☐ cut down ~	172
☐ be pleased to *do*	170		
☐ be proud of ~	142	**D**	
☐ be ready for ~	142	☐ day after day	172
☐ be ready to *do*	142	☐ day and night	172
☐ be satisfied with ~	170	☐ decide to *do*	144
☐ be scared of ~	170	☐ depend on ~	172
☐ be sick in bed	170	☐ die of ~	173
☐ be similar to ~	170	☐ do *one's* best	144
☐ be sorry for *doing*	170	☐ do *one's* homework	144
☐ be surprised at ~	143	☐ do well	144
☐ be surprised to *do*	171	☐ drive *A* home	173
✓ ☐ be tired from ~	171		
☐ be tired of *doing*	171	**E**	
☐ be worried about ~	143	☐ each other	144
☐ because of ~	171	☐ either *A* or *B*	173

☐ enjoy *doing*	145
☐ enjoy *oneself*	173
☐ (形容詞 / 副詞) enough for ~	145
☐ (形容詞 / 副詞) enough to *do*	145
☐ even if ~	173
☐ every other day	173
☐ exchange *A* for *B*	145

F

☐ fall asleep	173
☐ fall down	145
☐ fall in love with ~	173
☐ far away	174
☐ far from ~	174
☐ feel at home	174
☐ feel better	174
☐ feel like *doing*	174
☐ feel sick	174
☐ fill in ~	174
☐ fill up (with~)	174
☐ find out ~	145
☐ finish *doing*	145
☐ first of all	145
☐ for a long time	146
☐ for a minute	175
☐ for a while	175
☐ for example	146
☐ for fun	175
☐ for *oneself*	175
☐ for some time	175
☐ for the first time	146
☐ forget to *do*	175
☐ from *A* to *B*	146
☐ from abroad	175
☐ from beginning to end	175

G

☐ get a good grade	146
☐ get a perfect score	146
☐ get angry	176
☐ get away from ~	176
☐ get back (from ~)	176
☐ get better	176
☐ get cold	146
☐ get dark	146
☐ get excited	176
☐ get home	147
☐ get hungry	147
☐ get in ~	176
☐ get off (~)	147
☐ get on (~)	147
☐ get out of ~	176
☐ get to ~	147
☐ get well	176
☐ give *A* a ride	147
☐ give back ~	177
☐ give up *doing*	177
☐ go abroad	177
☐ go and *do*	147
☐ go away	177
☐ go back home	147
☐ go by	177
☐ go fishing	148
☐ go for a walk	148
☐ go home	148
☐ go into ~	177
☐ go on a tour	148
☐ go on a trip	148
☐ go out (for ~)	148
☐ go shopping	148
☐ go [walk] straight	148

- ☐ go to bed — 149
- ☐ go to see a movie — 149
- ☐ go to sleep — 177
- ☐ go to the doctor — 149
- ☐ go to work — 149
- ☐ graduate from ~ — 149
- ☐ grow up — 149

H

- ☐ had better *do* — 177
- ☐ happen to *do* — 178
- ☐ have a baby — 178
- ☐ have a chance to *do* — 149
- ☐ have a cold — 149
- ☐ have a dream — 178
- ☐ have a fight — 178
- ☐ have a good memory — 178
- ☐ have a good sleep — 178
- ☐ have a great time — 150
- ☐ have a stomachache — 178
- ☐ have a talk — 178
- ☐ have been to ~ — 150
- ☐ have enough (名詞) to *do* — 150
- ☐ have fun — 150
- ☐ have lunch — 150
- ☐ have never been to ~ — 150
- ☐ have no idea — 179
- ☐ have time to *do* — 150
- ☐ have to *do* — 150
- ☐ hear from ~ — 179
- ☐ hear of ~ — 179
- ☐ help *A* with ~ — 179
- ☐ how far ~ — 179
- ☐ how long ~ — 151
- ☐ how many times ~ — 151
- ☐ how often ~ — 151
- ☐ how to *do* — 151
- ☐ hundreds of ~ — 179
- ☐ hurry up — 151

I

- ☐ I'd like to *do* — 151
- ☐ in a circle — 179
- ☐ in a group — 179
- ☐ in a minute — 180
- ☐ in fact — 180
- ☐ in front of ~ — 151
- ☐ in *one's* opinion — 151
- ☐ in peace — 180
- ☐ in public — 180
- ☐ in return — 180
- ☐ in spite of ~ — 180
- ☐ in the end — 180
- ☐ in the middle of ~ — 152
- ☐ in the morning [afternoon, evening] — 152
- ☐ in the world — 152
- ☐ in those days — 180
- ☐ in time (for ~) — 181
- ☐ instead of ~ — 181
- ☐ introduce *A* to *B* — 181
- ☐ invite *A* to *B* — 152
- ☐ It is (形容詞) for *A* to *do* — 152
- ☐ It takes *A* (時間) to *do* — 152

K

- ☐ keep in touch with ~ — 181
- ☐ keep *one's* promise — 181

L

- [ ] last week [month, year] 152
- [ ] laugh at ~ 152
- [ ] leave A at home 153
- [ ] leave a message 153
- [ ] lie down 181
- [ ] like this 181
- [ ] little by little 181
- [ ] look after ~ 182
- [ ] look around (~) 153
- [ ] look for ~ 153
- [ ] look forward to *doing* [A] 153
- [ ] look like ~ 182
- [ ] look out of ~ 182
- [ ] look up ~ 182
- [ ] look well 153
- [ ] lose *one's* way 182
- [ ] lots of ~ 153

M

- [ ] make A from B 182
- [ ] make A into B 182
- [ ] make A of B 182
- [ ] make a mistake 183
- [ ] make (a) noise 183
- [ ] make a speech 153
- [ ] make money 183
- [ ] more than ~ 154
- [ ] most of ~ 154
- [ ] move to ~ 154

N

- [ ] name A after B 183
- [ ] near here 154
- [ ] need to *do* 154
- [ ] neither A nor B 183
- [ ] next door 183
- [ ] next time 183
- [ ] next to ~ 183
- [ ] no more (名詞) 184
- [ ] not ~ at all 154
- [ ] not A but B 184
- [ ] not ~ yet 154
- [ ] not have to *do* 154
- [ ] not only A but also B 155

O

- [ ] on business 155
- [ ] on foot 184
- [ ] on *one's* [the] right 155
- [ ] on *one's* [the] way home 155
- [ ] on *one's* [the] way to ~ 155
- [ ] on the other hand 184
- [ ] on time 184
- [ ] on vacation 184
- [ ] on weekends 155
- [ ] once a day [week, month] 184
- [ ] once more 184
- [ ] one after another 185
- [ ] one another 185
- [ ] One is ~, the other is ... 185
- [ ] one more (名詞) 155
- [ ] one of ~ 155
- [ ] one of the+(形容詞の最上級)+(複数名詞) 156
- [ ] over there 156

P

- [ ] pass the [an] exam 156
- [ ] pick up ~ 156

☐ plan to *do*	185
☐ prepare for ~	185
☐ put on ~	156

R

☐ receive a prize	156
☐ right away	185
☐ right now	156
☐ run away	156

S

☐ save money	157
☐ say goodbye	185
☐ say hello to ~	157
☐ say to *oneself*	185
☐ see *A* off	186
☐ shake hands with ~	157
☐ shout at ~	157
☐ show *A* around ~	186
☐ show *A* how to *do*	157
☐ sleep well	186
☐ slow down	186
☐ smile at ~	186
☐ so (形容詞 / 副詞) that ~	157
☐ so far	186
☐ so many ~	186
☐ some other time	186
☐ something (形容詞)	157
☐ something (形容詞) to *do*	187
☐ something to *do*	157
☐ sound like ~	187
☐ speak to ~	187
☐ spend *A* on ~	158
☐ stand for ~	187
☐ start with ~	187
☐ stay home	158
☐ stay up late	158
☐ stay with ~	187
☐ stop by	187
☐ such a [an] (形容詞) (名詞)	158
☐ such as ~	187
☐ suffer from ~	188
☐ surf (on) the Internet	188

T

☐ take *A* to *B*	158
☐ take a break	188
☐ take a look at ~	188
☐ take (a) medicine	188
☐ take a picture	158
☐ take a rest	188
☐ take a seat	188
☐ take a trip	188
☐ take a walk	189
☐ take care of ~	158
☐ take lessons	158
☐ take off	159
☐ take off ~	159
☐ take out ~	189
☐ take part in ~	159
☐ talk on the phone	159
☐ tell *A* how to *do*	159
☐ tell *A* to *do*	159
☐ tell a lie	189
☐ (比較級) than any other (単数名詞)	189
☐ than usual	159
☐ thank *A* for ~	189
☐ the other day	159
☐ these days	189

- ☐ think about *doing* 160
- ☐ think of ~ 160
- ☐ this is *one's* first time to *do* 189
- ☐ this morning 160
- ☐ this way 189
- ☐ thousands of ~ 190
- ☐ throw away ~ 160
- ☐ ~ times as (形容詞) as *A* 190
- ☐ too (形容詞/副詞) to *do* 160
- ☐ travel to ~ 160
- ☐ try on ~ 160
- ☐ turn ~ over 190
- ☐ turn down ~ 160
- ☐ turn left [right] 161
- ☐ turn off ~ 161
- ☐ turn on ~ 161
- ☐ turn up ~ 161
- ☐ twice a month [week, day] 161

U
- ☐ used to *do* 190

V
- ☐ visit [see] *A* in the hospital 161

W
- ☐ wait for ~ 161
- ☐ wake up 161
- ☐ walk along ~ 162
- ☐ walk around 190
- ☐ want *A* to *do* 162
- ☐ want to be [become] 162
- ☐ what to *do* 162
- ☐ when to *do* 162
- ☐ where to *do* 162
- ☐ work well 162
- ☐ would love to *do* 190
- ☐ write down ~ 190
- ☐ write to ~ 190

Y
- ☐ ~ year(s) old 162

会話表現編

A
- ☐ Are you all right? 196
- ☐ Are you ready to order? 196

C
- ☐ Can I take a message? 196
- ☐ Can you help me with ~? 196
- ☐ Can you tell me where [when / why / who など] ~? 196
- ☐ Certainly. 196
- ☐ Congratulations! 197

D
- ☐ Do you think so? 197

E
- ☐ Excuse me. 197

G
- ☐ Good job. / You did a great job. 197
- ☐ Good luck. 197
- ☐ Guess what? 197

H
- ☐ Have a good time. 198
- ☐ Have a nice trip. 198
- ☐ Help yourself to ~. 198
- ☐ Here it is. 198
- ☐ Here you are. 198
- ☐ Here's ~. 198
- ☐ Hold on. 199
- ☐ How [What] about ~? 199
- ☐ How about *doing* ~? 199
- ☐ How about you? 199
- ☐ How do [did] you like ~? 199
- ☐ How is [was] ~? 199
- ☐ How long does it take to *do* ~? 200

I
- ☐ I beg your pardon? 200
- ☐ I can't wait. 200
- ☐ I don't think so. 200
- ☐ I hear ~. 200
- ☐ I hope ~. 200
- ☐ I hope so. 201
- ☐ I see. 201
- ☐ I think so, too. 201
- ☐ I'd be glad [happy] to. 201
- ☐ I'd love to. 201
- ☐ I'll be right back. 201
- ☐ I'll be there. 202
- ☐ I'll think about it. 202
- ☐ I'm afraid (that) ~. 202
- ☐ I'm afraid I can't. 202
- ☐ I'm afraid not. 202
- ☐ I'm coming. 202
- ☐ I'm full. 203
- ☐ I'm glad you like it. 203
- ☐ I'm just looking. 203
- ☐ I'm not from here. 203
- ☐ I'm not sure. 203
- ☐ I'm sure ~. 203
- ☐ Is anything wrong? 204
- ☐ It looks like rain. 204
- ☐ It's my pleasure. 204
- ☐ It's time for ~. 204

- ☐ It's time to *do* ~. 204

J
- ☐ Just a moment [minute]. 204

L
- ☐ Let me see. 205

M
- ☐ May [Can] I help you? 205
- ☐ Me, too. 205

N
- ☐ Nice talking to you. 205
- ☐ Nice to see you again. 205
- ☐ No, not really. 205
- ☐ No, not yet. 206
- ☐ No problem. 206
- ☐ No, thanks [thank you]. 206

O
- ☐ Of course. 206
- ☐ Of course not. 206

P
- ☐ (Please) take your time. 206

S
- ☐ Same to you. 207
- ☐ See you later. 207
- ☐ So do [am] I. 207
- ☐ Something is wrong with ~. 207
- ☐ Sounds good [nice, great]. 207
- ☐ Sure. 207

T
- ☐ Take care. 208
- ☐ Thanks anyway. 208
- ☐ Thanks [Thank you] for *doing* ~. 208
- ☐ (That) sounds like fun. 208
- ☐ That would be great [nice]. 208
- ☐ That's a good idea. 208
- ☐ That's all. 209
- ☐ That's fine (with ~). 209
- ☐ That's right. 209
- ☐ That's too bad. 209
- ☐ That's very kind of you. 209
- ☐ This is ~. 209

W
- ☐ What do you do? 210
- ☐ What do you think of ~? 210
- ☐ What happened? 210
- ☐ What would you like (for ~)? 210
- ☐ What's the matter with ~? 210
- ☐ What's the problem? 210
- ☐ What's up? 211
- ☐ What's wrong with ~? 211
- ☐ Why don't we ~? 211
- ☐ Why don't you ~? 211
- ☐ Why not? 211
- ☐ Would you like to *do* ~? 211

Y
- ☐ Yes, speaking. 212
- ☐ You can do it. 212
- ☐ (You) go ahead. 212
- ☐ You're welcome. 212